THE CLOWNING WORKBOOK

OTHER TITLES IN THE THEATRE ARTS WORKBOOKS SERIES:

The Dramatic Text Workbook and Video: Practical Tools for Actors and Directors by David Carey and Rebecca Clark Carey

The Actor's Workbook: A Practical Guide to Training, Rehearsing and Devising + Video by Alex Clifton

Stage Combat Arts: An Integrated Approach to Acting, Voice and Text Work + Video by Christopher DuVal

Directing with the Michael Chekhov Technique: A Workbook with Video for Directors, Teachers and Actors by Mark Monday

The Laban Workbook for Actors: A Practical Training Guide with Video by Katya Bloom, Barbara Adrian, Tom Casciero, Jennifer Mizenko and Claire Porter

The Shakespeare Workbook and Video by David Carey and Rebecca Clark Carey

THE CLOWNING WORKBOOK

A Practical Course

JON DAVISON

Series editors: David Carey and
Rebecca Clark Carey

LONDON • NEW YORK • OXFORD • NEW DELHI • SYDNEY

METHUEN DRAMA
Bloomsbury Publishing Plc
50 Bedford Square, London, WC1B 3DP, UK
1385 Broadway, New York, NY 10018, USA
29 Earlsfort Terrace, Dublin 2, Ireland

BLOOMSBURY, METHUEN DRAMA and the Methuen Drama logo are
trademarks of Bloomsbury Publishing Plc

First published in Great Britain 2023

Copyright © Jon Davison, 2023

Jon Davison has asserted his right under the Copyright, Designs and Patents Act,
1988, to be identified as author of this work.

For legal purposes the Acknowledgements on p. xii constitute an extension of
this copyright page.

Cover design: Charlotte Daniels
Cover image © Ieva Aust

All rights reserved. No part of this publication may be reproduced or transmitted
in any form or by any means, electronic or mechanical, including photocopying,
recording, or any information storage or retrieval system, without prior
permission in writing from the publishers.

Bloomsbury Publishing Plc does not have any control over, or responsibility for,
any third-party websites referred to or in this book. All internet addresses given
in this book were correct at the time of going to press. The author and publisher
regret any inconvenience caused if addresses have changed or sites have ceased
to exist, but can accept no responsibility for any such changes.

A catalogue record for this book is available from the British Library.

ISBN: HB: 978-1-3500-5045-7
       PB: 978-1-3500-5047-1
       ePDF: 978-1-3500-5043-3
       eBook: 978-1-3500-5049-5

Series: Theatre Arts Workbooks

Typeset by RefineCatch Limited, Bungay, Suffolk
Printed and bound in Great Britain

To find out more about our authors and books visit www.bloomsbury.com
and sign up for our newsletters.

CONTENTS

List of illustrations xi
Acknowledgements xii
Preface xv

Introduction 1

PART ONE 'THAT WAS FUNNY' 11

1   Introductions and warm-ups 13

1.1   Names and naming 15
1.2   Wrong naming 20
Case study 1.1 Clown workshop at AFDA, Johannesburg,
April 2018 25
Case study 1.2 Clowning and Puppetry workshop, London,
April 2019 28

2   Name Tag 31

2.1   Name Tag as a game 31
2.2   Laughter response 36
2.3   Forgetting about the game 38
Case study 2.1 Clown workshop for dancers, London,
June 2017 39
Case study 2.2 Clown workshop at AFDA, Johannesburg,
April 2018 40

vi CONTENTS

Case study 2.3 Undergraduate Physical Theatre students, University of Stellenbosch, South Africa, March 2018 42

Case study 2.4 BA European Theatre Arts students and graduates, Rose Bruford College, London, September 2017 42

3 Ball play 47

3.1 Throw and catch 47

Case study 3.1 Clown workshop, Ngizwe Youth Theatre, Soweto, April 2018 53

Case study 3.2 Clown workshops for primary school teachers in service training day, Southend, UK, September 2018 54

Case study 3.3 Open public workshop at Victoria & Albert Museum 'Friday Late', April 2018 55

Case study 3.4 MA Voice Studies, RCSSD, London, May 2018 56

4 Doing things when it's funny 61

4.1 Throw the ball when it's funny 61

4.2 Stop when it's funny 69

Case study 4.1 Clowning and Puppetry workshop, London, April 2019 72

5 On/Off 75

5.1 Ball-Clap-Hit 75

5.2 Leave or stay 78

5.3 Leave when not funny 79

5.4 On/Off with scripts 82

6 Step-Laugh 87

6.1 Step-Laugh – crossing the stage 87

6.2 Step-Laugh scripts 90

Case study 6.1 Weekly clown course, London Clown School, June 2019 91

Case study 6.2 Five-day workshop, Brussels, November 2019 95

CONTENTS

Case study 6.3 Weekend workshop, Brighton November 2019 95

Case study 6.4 Clowning and puppetry workshop, April 2019, London 97

Case study 6.5 DH Ensemble, April 2019, London 98

Case study 6.6 MA Shakespeare Studies, Shakespeare's Globe, London, December 2009 99

7 That was/n't funny 101

7.1 Catching the ball in a circle 101
7.2 Catching the ball for an audience 102
7.3 Any action in a circle 102
7.4 Any action for an audience 103
7.5 This is going to be funny 103
7.6 Extended variations 104

Case study 7.1 Weekend workshop, Brussels, November 2019 105

Case study 7.2 Calgary Clown Festival, Canada, September 2019 107

8 Make others into clowns 111

8.1 Throw ball with intention 111
8.2 Don't catch it when it's funny 112

Case study 8.1 London Metropolitan University, BA Theatre and Performance, 2019 114

Case study 8.2 London Clown School weekly class, 2019 114

9 Laughter as a pardon 117

9.1 Ball Tag 118
9.2 Musical Chairs 121
9.3 Grandmother's Footsteps with laughter conditioning 122

Case study 9.1 AFDA, Johannesburg, one-week workshop March 2018 123

Case study 9.2 Circus Hub, Nottingham, series of weekend workshops, July 2018 124

viii CONTENTS

10 Conclusions to Part One: Right and wrong thinking 127

PART TWO 'I FEEL FUNNY' 131

11 I (don't) feel funny 135

    11.1   I caught the ball 135

    11.2   Free scripts 137

    11.3   'This is going to be funny' 138

    11.4   Homework 139

    Case study 11.1 Week workshop, AFDA, Johannesburg, April 2018 141

    Case study 11.2 Week workshop, Brussels, July 2019 145

    Case study 11.3 Weekly clown course, London Clown School, January 2020 146

12 Self-laughter 149

    12.1   Basic mirror self-laughter – solo 149

    12.2   Mirror laughter plus free action 151

    Case study 12.1 Weekend workshop, Gent, Belgium, February 2018 152

    Case study 12.2 BA Theatre and Performance Practice, London Metropolitan University, November 2019 154

    Case study 12.3 MA Voice Studies, RCSSD, London, May 2018 155

13 Reading others' feelings 161

    13.1   Doing the expected 161

    13.2   Doing what the audience expects 163

14 Guess the show 165

    14.1   Solo performance 165

    14.2   Duo performance 167

    14.3   Trio shows 168

    14.4   Audience variations 168

CONTENTS

Case study 14.1 Week workshop, University of the Arts, Cape Town, February 2017 169

Case study 14.2 BA Theatre and Performance Practice, London Metropolitan University, November 2019 171

15 Feeling shit 173

Case study 15.1 Comedy Module, BA Drama, Liverpool John Moores University, October 2017 174

16 Personal clown skills 175

16.1 Self-reflection 175

16.2 Sharing your reflections 176

16.3 Teaching your knowledge 176

Case study 16.1 Research workshop, Clown Symposium 'State of Play', Edge Hill University, December 2018 177

16.4 Clowning socially 178

PART THREE 'THAT WAS SUPPOSED TO BE FUNNY' 179

17 Funny plans 181

17.1 Make a funny plan 181

17.2 On-script and off-script 184

17.3 Plans with feelings 185

17.4 Types of plan 186

Case study 17.1 Devising class, London Clown School, May 2019 188

Case study 17.2 Public open workshop, Victoria & Albert Museum 'Friday Late', April 2018 189

17.5 Funny plans and simple scripts 189

18 Intruders 193

18.1 Intrude on an organized performance 193

18.2 Reverse intrusion 196

18.3   Classical clowning 197

18.4   Multiple intrusions 198

Case study 18.1 BA European Theatre Arts students and
graduates, Rose Bruford College, London, September
2017 200

19   Clowns in plays 209

Case study 19.1 Clowning and Shakespeare, Drama School
– Estonian Academy of Music and Theatre / Rose Bruford
College, February 2020 209

19.1   Richard Tarlton 210

19.2   Will Kemp 216

Notes 227

Bibliography of works cited 243

Index 247

Visit the following website for access to a range of videos that
accompany the exercises outlined in this text:

**www.bloomsburyonlineresources.com/the-clowning-
workbook-a-practical-course**

The video links are named according to the paragraph in the
book where the exercise shown in the video is described. All
videos were recorded during a workshop held at George Enescu
National University of Arts in Iaşi, Romania, 17–19 December
2021.

ILLUSTRATIONS

1   That Was Funny: Athena Amoret, Kaisa Koskinen, Jum Faruq   30

2   That Was Funny: Bienam Perez, Jum Faruq, Giedre Degutyte   46

3   On/Off: Kaisa Koskinen entering the stage   60

4   On/Off: Jum Faruq entering the stage   74

5   Step-Laugh: Kaisa Koskinen crossing the space   86

6   Three on a Bench: Athena Amoret, Giedre Degutyte, Kaisa Koskinen   110

7   I Feel Funny: Jon Davison   148

8   Mirror Laugh: Camille Suarez   160

9   I Feel Stupid: Giedre Degutyte   172

10   That Was Supposed to Be Funny: Kaisa Koskinen, Camille Suarez   192

All photos by: Ieva Aust

ACKNOWLEDGEMENTS

Thanks to all the students and participants in the workshops I have run over the past few years, in specialized and mixed groups, who have discovered so much new knowledge.

The BA European Theatre Arts students and graduates at Rose Bruford found out how clowns can intrude on dramatic spaces created by others – and not just in the traditional dramatic fictions we are accustomed to (think Shakespeare's clowns), but also into ensemble visual performance of the most abstract nature.

The undergraduates of the BA Theatre and Performance Practices at London Metropolitan discovered new exercises exploring their own clown knowledge born of hugely varied experiences, a clowning defined both personally and by social conditions.

The teenagers of Ngizwe Youth Theatre in Soweto discovered that adding applause to laughter builds positive feelings about our own failures in front of our peers, and boosting their ability to make fools of themselves for fun.

The students on the MA Performance Practice as Research at RCSSD discovered how clowning is not only a performance practice in its own right, but can also be employed as a research methodology, ideal for questioning assumptions, suggesting surprising hypotheses and showing the way to glean new knowledge from failure.

Primary school teachers on Learning in Harmony Trust INSET day in Southend revealed surprising conclusions about who might be more or less predisposed to clowning, suggesting new ways to engage clowning students from backgrounds of privilege and non-privilege.

The MA Voice Studies students at Royal Central School of Speech and Drama discovered how clowning can cultivate a positive approach

ACKNOWLEDGEMENTS

to the fear which inhibits free production of sound, beginning with laughter but ending with the whole voice.

BA Physical Theatre students at Stellenbosch University took possession of the knowledge that moving forwards puts you in constant danger of making mistakes, coining the new clown training technical term 'backsy'.

Deaf and hearing performers, working together in the DH Ensemble and in workshops, discovered how clowning's approach to staging inequality offers an exciting means of addressing diversity in celebratory ways.

Both students and staff at AFDA (Africa Film Drama Art) in Johannesburg, working together with mature professional performers, discovered that taking on board the dynamics of clowning means letting go of the rules and principles of other genres, from improv to musical comedy, leading to unheard of outcomes, and that clowning is its own genre.

Drop-in participants at the ongoing clowning workshop in the middle of the Victoria & Albert Museum's exhibition spaces discovered how easy clowning is, that we already hold clown knowledge, and that clowns thrive in places of high culture.

Students on workshops in Gent and Brussels in Belgium (re)discovered their national and international differences through the magnifying and distorting prism of clowning, discovering new ways to find themselves ridiculous in the eyes of their neighbours.

The MA Shakespeare Studies students discovered how easy it is to appear ridiculous on the stage at the Globe, a space whose design eases the actor into dynamic interaction with the audience, and is a natural space for clowns.

The students at City Varsity in Cape Town discovered ways, as clowns, that we can stage real life events that most repel us, transforming the news stories we don't want to read about into digestible yet potent form, enabling a conversation that is inclusive even on subjects that divide nations.

Workshop attendees at the Montreal Clown Festival not only discovered yet another distinct approach to clown teaching to add to their nation's already thriving clown education, but also discovered the perfect Canadian clown exercise, combining diligence and humility.

New York Clown Theater Festival clown workshop participants discovered how to summarize the principles of clowning, rendering the artform swift and easy to grasp, producing complex performance ideas that grabbed even the festival's clown experts.

BA and BTech circus students at Circomedia in Bristol discovered that clowning doesn't mean ruining or underperforming the skill that you worked so hard to achieve, and that there are countless ways to frame your performance in order to appear ridiculous and virtuosic at the same time.

Students of puppetry in an open workshop discovered that there are many permutations of puppet, clown, performer and object, and that audience's laughter can drive puppets just as it can humans, with the advantage (or disadvantage) that puppets won't feel bad about their failure to be funny.

'State of Play' Clown Symposium participants at Edge Hill University discovered new exercises to be used in clown training, based on personal experiences of social marginalization, suggesting that clowns can be defined as social figures rather than inhabiting inner selves.

BA students in workshops at Liverpool John Moores University discovered how clowning principles can be appropriated for their own artistic ends, individually and as companies, and that clowning includes a vast range of aesthetic styles.

Students from the Estonian Academy of Music and Theatre visiting Rose Bruford College, London, for a six-week Exploring Shakespeare intensive, explored innovatory practical means to stage clowning from early modern theatre.

Undergraduates, postgraduates and lecturers in performing arts and other arts fields at the George Enescu National University of Arts in Iași, Romania, found how they could incorporate focusing on their own subjective experiences as actors into a traditional conservatoire-style arts training.

And students on the regular weekly classes at London Clown School have been continuously discovering, testing and developing a whole range of new clown training exercises based on laughter response, simplifying the process of learning clown and contributing to the demystification of the artform.

PREFACE

Here is a group of students. They are together to study theatre and performance in a big city university. They are diverse, not just in terms of social background, ethnicity, first language, gender, disability, age or sexual orientation, but also in their artistic priorities and interests. One wants to be a screen actor, one dreams of forming a devising company and writing and directing, one is passionate about plays dealing with serious issues, one wants to use drama to work with real-life trauma. Another has found an affinity and aptitude for physical, visual theatre, another for cabaret, others for drag, circus, street dance. What will be their experience of clowning? How will clowning intersect with and impact on their own concerns and practices?

Happily, even a cursory glance at clowning historically and cross-culturally reveals a plurality of form, purpose, technique and philosophy. The existence of clowns and clowning is embedded in the history of theatre and our wider cultures. Sometimes it is a distinct performance mode alongside others as in Shakespeare or Victorian melodrama, sometimes it is a source for new conceptualizations of theatre such as with Beckett or Ionesco, sometimes it is a prime source for whole methods of acting as in Brecht's Gestus and distance effect. In many cases clowning weaves itself right through a web of comic registers and modes, in pantomime, cabaret, sitcoms, stand-up or digital media.

Hence, that student of film acting might find, in the irreverent freedom of clowns to do whatever they want, the spark needed to bring to life the most technical of shots. Or that writer/deviser might find how the relationship between script, actors and the moment of performance in front of an audience might be planned and prepared for but also made flexible to the surprises of the live event. Or the drama therapist might discover how clowning gives permission to share

xvi   **PREFACE**

stories that our fear of presenting ourselves as victims would otherwise repress.

We might see how clowning supports not only the student who feels they can excel only in non-speaking performance, but also the one whose ideas come to them as lightning bolts of text, complex backstories full of bizarre characters, or as a chaotic collage of actions and images. Then there is the class clown. Every time they try to play serious with their classmates, everyone cracks up laughing. They despair. But fear not, for they are a clown. You don't need an aptitude for clowning nor an interest in it to benefit greatly. And you don't have to be one of the so-called 'real' clowns.[1] There is no 'ideal clown student'. Some are energetic, fearless or conscientious. But others are lazy, distracted or shy! 'The' clown doesn't exist.

In this variegated universe of forms, styles, identities, contexts, backgrounds and aesthetics, what kind of method of training could be suitably flexible whilst maintaining some kind of vision appropriate to the particular and peculiar demands of clowning?

This book is written from experiences of teaching a range of groups around the world, with that question constantly in the background. Those teaching experiences have sometimes led me to question and change my approaches, when my own habits or assumptions ceased to function in new environments, cultures or specialized settings. They have also led me to search for what might remain constant in clowning for us today in a globalized yet diverse world. In each place or in each group, whether seemingly homogeneous or apparently mixed, there does appear to be a delight to discover how exciting it feels to clown, to be the one who says to us: 'No problem, you can laugh at me!' But this depends on all kinds of factors: what your expectations are, how you feel about looking ridiculous in front of the people present, what is deemed funny in your culture, how others see you, whether you are ambitious to perform or not, whether your experiences have taught you how to survive on the margins, or to assume advantages. In other words, this will vary according to time, place, and who you find yourself with.

For some time now, I have realized that my own teaching works as a kind of 'thinking in action', as my way of trying to figure out how this thing called a clown works. Obviously, as a professional who is paid to do a job, I endeavour to pass on to the best of my ability any knowledge I have garnered and that may be of use to students. But also, inevitably,

PREFACE

xvii

I am led to experiment, to ask questions about my own practice as a teacher, about clowning, about how different participants respond differently. The last few years have been no exception in this sense. They have been characterized by a certain crystallization of some of my thinking and practices, the result of which has been a more or less consistent body of exercises designed to simplify and clarify the learning process of clowning.

In many ways, this book is the result of this research. It presents outcomes, the exercises, at this particular point in time, but also aims to explore just how and why those outcomes have come to be formed. This is not especially radical. It's a pattern we can find in many examples of performer training from Stanislavski[2] to Lecoq.[3]

These comparisons are not just a way to show that clowning operates at a level as complex as the 'monuments' of acting history. They also hopefully bring those monuments down to earth, where they seem just like us, asking questions because we don't know how to do it but are passionate enough about it to dedicate time and energy to finding something out.

This adventurous spirit and a courage to take risks will serve us well in pretty much any context we will find ourselves in. Some of the most exciting explorers of actor training put such attitudes at the heart of their work. An actor who worked with Joan Littlewood tells a story about her throwing a script at them and saying,

> 'Right I want you to read all the parts. What? But I want to read the part . . . No I want you to read all of them: men, women, children, old men, young women.' And he did and felt ridiculous and probably looked ridiculous [. . .] She wanted actors with that curiosity and a willingness to play and take risks. If you weren't prepared to do some training then what was the point? The spirit of experimentation was important.
>
> HOLDSWORTH 2017

That old question – 'what's the point of this?' – may come equally from a young student keen to learn or a seasoned professional actor wary of new challenges.

Many of the exercises in this book toy with what we tell ourselves is the right way to do things, with rules, with norms, whether explicit or not. Beginning with a rule-bound game, what ways can we find to step away from the limitations of rules and explore our freedom to break, to contravene and to ignore them? How might we produce clowning when we drop our insistence on 'playing by the rules', or being 'fair'? Can we find a new kind of freedom where the fun is to be had from a detachment from what is expected of us, learned patterns of behaviour are dispensed with, and physical habits are contradicted – when a fear of being unfair is dumped and the joy of the unbalanced energizes our performance?

Much clown training over the past half century has leaned heavily on games and play which, especially in Britain, has held a dominant position since precisely those experiments by Littlewood. But have we become too accustomed to such methods? All methods date eventually. Yesterday's open-ended experiment easily morphs into today's orthodoxy, where lineage trumps usefulness and truth-claims appear more attractive than asking honest questions. Play and games certainly resonated 50 years ago in a society still burdened by rigid social structures, and of course it might be fun for the performer, but what happens if we leave rules aside for a moment? What other mechanisms could productively drive our clowning today?

INTRODUCTION

This book is concerned with laughter, and the unique relationship the clown performer has with it – when it is present and when it is absent. But it is not concerned directly with the question of HOW to be funny. Nor is it concerned with the question of WHY something is funny. These are not inane questions but they have been dealt with amply by others elsewhere.

I have been teaching clowning for 30 years. It all started for me when, as a student of clown, I and some classmates got together to repeat our favourite exercises and gain some extra practice. I began to come up with variations on the exercises, looking for ways to work out how to understand further what clowning was and how to do it. Previous to discovering clowning, I had spent several years immersed in 'serious' acting, but had never had the urge to study it or to explore why what I did worked (or didn't work). Years later, when I came to teach in drama schools, I realized why I hadn't been drawn to that training, which foregrounded the imagination, the building of a character, the backstory – all skills which I did not possess and had no interest in acquiring. My enthusiasm was for acting as action, where the meaning follows on and the interpretation is in the hands of the audience, not the actor.

Those early experimental explorations into clown learning led quickly on to having a body of new exercises that I then found I could teach to others. But the exploratory drive remained. Nothing ever felt definitive, just maybe a new step towards further understanding. The exercises in this book are one more step on that path. They are my latest attempt to condense the training into the simplest and most accessible form I can. My concern has always been to simplify. Clowning is sometimes spoken about in mysterious tones, with allusions to depths of meaning. Those may be valid conclusions to draw, but they don't, in my experience, serve as useful starting points on the journey. We cannot aim directly for such grandiose or abstract goals. My own personal struggle to learn and understand clowning was a constant encounter with such obstacles, the concepts which have become orthodoxies over the past half century since Jacques Lecoq's experiments: the 'inner clown', the 'personal clown', 'authenticity', or the very notion of '*the* clown' (rather than 'a clown' or 'this clown here'). These difficulties are what have driven me to search incessantly by means of my teaching. If it had been easy, then it would never have occurred to me to ask 'how do we do it?'

To be fair on Lecoq, he was by all accounts just asking questions as well. But he was asking those questions, and getting his answers, in his own time and place. That time and place saw old French and European circus clowns as irrelevant. In post-war France and beyond, meaning would be sought not in history or tradition (who would look to the past for answers then, when the recent past was so horrific and laden with guilt?) but in the present, just as Sartre's existentialism, Beckett's absurdism and a host of artistic practices grounded in spontaneity would be doing throughout the 1950s and 1960s. But we are in a different time and place and our references and our moment are different.

In place of that idealistic yearning for a universalism of the individual to be discovered within us, today we live in societies acutely aware of our cultural differences and the structural inequalities which define our identities. The one-size-fits-all approach of 'finding one's clown', through a method where the teacher takes on the role of boss clown (whether playfully or cruelly is irrelevant) in order to put the student into a place of vulnerability, or 'in the shit', is a product of those times past. Actually, though, as a cis het non-disabled white male, this method is not really a challenge to me as a student. Once the class is over, I can go back to the outside world knowing I am privileged to be pretty invulnerable. But I am no longer comfortable playing this game that expects students without that privilege (black, women, disabled, trans) to engage with this 'whiteface clown' teacher who is there to make them feel yet more powerless. There is no need to continue to believe that we can only clown from this feeling of powerlessness. We could equally clown from anger, or from joy, or from a desire to celebrate.

But, back to what is in this book, not what isn't.

The exercises presented here might sometimes seem so simple as to appear mechanical. Indeed, I have encouraged this perspective,

INTRODUCTION

describing the tasks as simple bits of work that anyone can carry out, so-called unskilled labour, as a way of diluting the fear that can arise when the student (or professional) is faced with the prospect of being in front of an audience (and in addition without the protection of a fictional character or setting). My intention is, by extracting the difficulty from the exercises, we can use them to explore our actual reality on stage (by 'stage' I mean any context where I find myself being watched by another, from Shakespeare's Globe to a chance encounter with a stranger in a shop queue). This reality on stage is one full of emotions, sensations and thoughts. By focusing on the simple tasks, we can become more aware of our responses on all these levels. Simple meditation techniques work in a similar way, recognizing that we cannot banish or 'stop' thinking or feeling, but we can change our perspective on ourselves. In fact, these emotions, sensations and thoughts will make up much of the content of a clown performance, in the absence of an authored, fictional character or narrative (and mostly I regard clowning as inhabiting this 'fiction-less' world). Once we start to come to grips with this material, we can see how clowns can create many different kinds of dynamic relationships between themselves, and between themselves and the public.

Most of these exercises are built upon the premise that when we begin to pay particular attention, as a performer, to our audience's response (and, later, to our own response), then exciting results will follow. Given that clowning as a genre is largely defined by our assumption that the clowns will be funny (and even Lecoq started from that same premise[1]) then that attention focuses on the laughter response. This then produces very particular and unique outcomes in clown performance which we will not find elsewhere. That is the simplest argument for at least some of us dedicating ourselves to such a task! And of course that doesn't mean we will always laugh.

By prioritizing this audience–performer relationship, this book clearly hopes to explore and develop the performer's awareness, skills and resources in clowning as an interactive genre. But, as we shall see, it will also entail experimenting with how you, as a performer, respond to that response from the onlooker. How do you behave, feel or think when the spectator laughs, or does not laugh? Indeed, how do you behave, feel or think upon the mere appearing in front of that audience whose expectations are already formed by the genre of performance on offer?

Such self-explorations are at the heart of acting in any genre, especially those which separate the roles of performer and spectator, where the former owns the rights to the stage and the latter are expected to occupy the auditorium only. Focusing on how you, as a performer, respond to your own presence in front of a responding audience, can only enrich your work and enable a broader practical understanding and coming to terms with some of the common struggles that the majority of performers will face throughout their careers.

It seems evident that we would do well to dive into all this material which emerges in the act of performing (and not only in clown performance). This subjective experience of the actors in relation to each other and to audiences does also take place in non-clowning, albeit somewhat masked by those fictional elements of theatre. And so, for me, this comes full circle, and what I present in this book, although developed with clowns in mind in a very specialized context, comes to be of value for any kind of performer. It may then also fulfil my own unacknowledged desire for an actor training that, as a young actor, I myself would have enrolled in.

Not long ago, I was asked to come up with a new module in clowning for undergraduate students. This was the opportunity to articulate the methods, aims and objectives of the evolution in clown training that I was exploring. Looking at the previous module, it was evident that such updating had not been undertaken recently. The old syllabus, anchored in concepts from half a century ago, had to be left behind. Happily, this was exactly what the institution was searching for, as student response had been that this way of learning was out of touch, out of date and difficult to relate to.

This book, then, is both a document of recent developments and an invitation to explore still further, how clowning could make sense to us today. It is aimed at all students, teachers, and practitioners of the performing arts. Hopefully, it will serve all those studying, teaching, coaching or working in live performance generally, from naturalistic plays to family pantomimes, from circus to Shakespeare, or even when the audience feels remote or absent as in film or online digital media.

It mostly follows the progression of the teaching modules I have offered over the past five years or so coinciding with the research and development of the exercises included here. The dominant pattern during this time period has been termly courses, with two- or three-hour sessions taught

INTRODUCTION

5

weekly over a ten- or twelve-week term. It has also included, as before, intensive workshops over a weekend or week. The weekly courses have occurred at London Clown School and also as a new module at London Metropolitan University. The intensive workshops have happened in a wide variety of institutions, companies and countries. Some of the latter were set up with the express intention to push the research further, as well as documenting it for the purposes of this book.

The presentation of the exercises in this book generally follows a three-part format.
Each chapter concerns a type of exercise and its variants and applications.

Firstly comes the basic exercise which I present the students with and invite them to experience as many times as seems worthwhile and enjoyable.

Secondly come the variations. Some of these are tried and trusted, but often these get made up on the spot, as a direct response to the needs and interests of the group.

Thirdly, in this book I give some examples ('case studies') which are anecdotal and drawn from specific classes. These are a mix of dialogues between students and myself, together with commentaries and descriptions of particular instances of an exercise. As such, they may or may not directly apply to your own context, but the main point here is to see how to adapt and how to become relevant.

If exploratory teaching has one benefit, it's this adaptability. Starting from a simple question, such as 'what happens when someone walks across a stage but only when we laugh?' (the Step-Laugh exercise), we can explore many aspects of how audience and performer interact when the latter enters and exits a stage. This dynamic interaction can apply in a multitude of settings, types of venue, audience and clown performance styles. There is no 'ideal clown' to be imagined here.

Hopefully, we end up drawing some conclusions from this exploration, which is a kind of experiment (what happens if . . .?) in the tradition of the 'scientific method', where hypotheses are tested in a laboratory and results are then reflected upon. The most illuminating results are, I would say, the unexpected results, as these give us new data with which to construct new experiments. This is a very classical way of learning, of gaining new knowledge. But that knowledge is only ever provisional and applicable to our particular case. Next day it might not work out the same way. The science parallel is not a whimsical one: truth is never reached but useful outcomes are attainable, if only 'for the moment'.

So this is how I imagine this book being used. Test, self-test, observe results, try again, try a variation, reflect on what is useful for you, re-invent and so on. Of course, you may use it in an entirely unexpected way that is right for you, too. All good actor trainers know that the job is eminently empirical.[2]

Underlying this repeated structure in the presentation of the exercises are a handful of simple concepts, as follows.

The training is task-based.

What I mean by 'task' are two things. Firstly, that the student performer will always be asked to carry out tasks which are 'possible'. Why would anyone propose something impossible for an actor to carry out? David Mamet explains it this way:

> Then, the chosen goal must be accomplishable. Here is a simple test: anything less capable of being accomplished than 'open the window' is not and can't be an action. You've heard directors and teachers by the gross tell you, 'Come to grips with yourself,' 'Regain your self-esteem,' 'Use the space,' and myriad other pretty phrases which they and you, were surprised to find difficult to accomplish. They are not difficult. They are impossible. They don't mean anything. They are nonsense syllables, strung together by ourselves and others, and they mean 'Damned if I know, and damned if I can admit it.'
>
> MAMET 1998: 73

Secondly, I mean use the word 'task' in the more precisely defined sense which describes what the job of the performer is to do. The fundamental task of the performer, according to Elly Konijn, could be said to be that of placing themselves in front of an audience:

> The imagined situation into which the actor projects himself can at that moment not be urgent for the actor; certainly no more urgent than the actual task situation which puts him face to face with an audience.
>
> KONIJN 1997: 89

INTRODUCTION

This 'urgency' gives rise to a range of emotions and sensations in the performer which, for the actor playing a fictional character, far outweigh in strength or intensity any attempt to approximate to the 'fictional emotions' of a role:

> Increased excitement in the actor is not so much associated with the portrayed character-emotions as with acting per se.
>
> KONIJN 1997: 108

Clearly, these sensations, most typically 'stage fright' or a variety of types of elation/fear, may be channelled into whatever creative framework the performance requires. Indeed, these 'task emotions', as Konijn refers to them, which arise from the encounter with the actor's task of being on a stage in front of an audience, could even be the very driving force which energizes the performance and makes the fictional emotion of a role feel convincing, both to the audience and to the actor. But in the case of the clown, we do not generally need to concern ourselves with how to channel our own emotion into an imagined, created 'character'. So where does it go?

The role, or task, of a clown is fundamentally to be the 'laughter-object'.

Naturally, the task emotion (the feelings which arise when being on stage) will still be present. How will that emotion be conditioned by the task of the clown? What do I feel when I stand up in front of a group of people and invite them to laugh at me? Perhaps already, while reading these questions, you begin to notice a feeling emerging as you imagine yourself placed in that role?

Jerry Seinfeld's joke about stage fright is often quoted by public speaking coaches:

> According to most studies, people's number-one fear is public speaking. Number two is death. Death is number two! Now, this means to the average person, if you have to go to a funeral, you're better off in the casket than doing the eulogy.
>
> SEINFELD 1993[3]

Whether it's actually true that such a study was produced, or that such a finding is true, or that Seinfeld made it up in order to tell a good joke, the usefulness of the gag is unmissable if you are in the business of teaching people how to attain ease and to overcome their fear of being up there in front of an audience. Part of the reason why the joke is funny is that it seems to state a truth that we believe we are all aware of through our own subjective experience, which contrasts, perhaps embarrassingly, with what 'ought' to be the greatest of all fears. (The other reasons why the joke works are the allusion to Seinfeld's own situation of being the solo comedian up there, right at the moment of telling, in front of that audience; and, most importantly, the joke's impeccable structure.)

Being alone and surrounded by others, who are knowledgeable, who are doing the right thing and who are powerful whilst I, alone, am stupid, wrong and weak: who would willingly put themselves in such a position? The answer is a clown. But does that mean that clowning is some kind of act of self-harm? Or, conversely, an act of heroic courage? I would say it is neither. Quite simply because, although this mocking function of laughter from a group towards an individual (or more laughter-objects) appears as an aggression, the receipt of laughter also carries a different meaning which is of acceptance. Once you experience the pleasure of provoking laughter by means of displaying your own ridiculousness, you will want more. From this point onwards, clowning becomes a joy, leaving behind any of its possible origin that is modelled on suffering, victimhood or marginalization.

Grappling with your own stage emotions.

This process, then, implies two clear strands. Firstly, it will involve a certain amount of personal grappling with your own feelings which are provoked by the task of playing the clown. What will you feel when invited to take this role? And how will you navigate a route away from suffering and towards pleasure? For some, this process takes some time, for others it happens in a moment, or they have undergone it previous to encountering clowning in any formal way.

Conditioning the performer to audience response.

The second strand which is implied will scrutinize the mechanisms which underly the fundamental clown/audience relationship I have just described. What implications are there of prioritizing your role as being ridiculous for others? What must you pay attention to in order to remain in this relationship? And what should you not be concerned with? This part of the training will demand a certain conditioning of the

INTRODUCTION

9

performer such that, for example, the response to laughter or its absence becomes paramount. Consequently, concerns for narrative or believable fictional circumstances fade into the background. These are questions of 'genre', of how the clown is conceived of. In this sense, then, clown training will be more a matter of reconditioning our habitual thinking.

Clearly, these two strands (feeling and thinking) will be constantly interweaving and affecting each other. With that in mind, I have structured the book in a way that makes a certain sense to me at this moment.

Part One: 'That Was Funny', groups those exercises which mostly deal with training the performer's response to the audience. They begin with set-ups involving simple actions and progress to using more complex instructions, designed to explore the dynamics between clown and audience, and between clown performers themselves. This all involves refocusing our thinking and being objective about others' responses.

Part Two: 'I Feel Funny', groups those exercises which begin with the performer's own subjective experience of playing within the genre of clowning, and seek to cultivate and develop over time an awareness and capacity for navigating the complexities of the actor's job, which is to use oneself as one's tool. This section is concerned with our subjective experience, on managing the stage emotions, or feelings.

Both of these first two parts of the book concentrate primarily on the performers' work in front of the audience 'in the moment', as it were. The aims are to work on increasing the familiarity with the details of how clowning functions as a mode of performance, as and when it is happening.

Part Three: 'That Was Supposed to Be Funny', moves on to consider how facets of performance which do not occur 'in the moment' bear upon the work of the clown. In the main, this involves looking at how scripts, plans, scores or devised compositions, whether they be short gags or more elaborate acts or scenes, intersect upon the clown performer's onstage relationship with the audience. The question is an old one: what is the relationship between the prepared performance and the actual performance? How does the performer exist on the stage in the present whilst utilizing the pre-ordained, the written? Even, in classical terms, what is the relationship between the writer and the actor?

Hopefully, this structure will prove simple for all readers to use, whether you read through it in order or pick out sections that interest you most. It is a workbook, a manual whose prime reason to exist is its utility. However, no acting exercise is 'just' practical. All methods come with their own baggage. Behind each exercise are a whole lot of ideas and assumptions, about what we think we should be achieving as performers, how we conceive of the function of the actor, or clown, and how that function fits into a world view about individuals, societies and culture. Any manual of clowning exercises, for example, will contain these assumptions, or philosophy, even when not explicitly stated. I have preferred to state and declare my own assumptions and philosophical starting points whenever I can. After all, it was a kind of 'hidden ideology' that proved such an obstacle to me as a student of clowning being encouraged to 'search' for a 'personal' or 'inner' clown. In any case, in a book intended for practical use, whether in a formal educational institution or not, some minimum level of contextualization is called for, placing a conservatoire practice within its theoretical lineage. As well as tracing some of the ideology of clown training, this also enables the exercises to be placed within the broader context of performer training beyond clowning.

Without that ability to reflect on our own methods, we risk a false idea of universality being attached to our own preferences, excluding a range of experiences and processes in our urge to find an imagined 'truth'.

The nature of pedagogy is grounded in the questions of what to teach, why to teach it, and then how to teach it. The answers to these questions reveal a complicity of intentions, a foregrounding of particular histories, and a perpetuation of particular realities at the expense of others.

> In a perfect world, we would like to believe that our acting classrooms contain culturally diverse theories and approaches to replicating humanity [. . .] Yet, this is not the case.
>
> LUCKETT and SHAFFER 2017: 1

PART ONE

'THAT WAS FUNNY'

1
INTRODUCTIONS AND WARM-UPS

All training exercises carry with them a whole set of assumed ideas about the task to be done. Our fundamental task is to train the performer. But the training of the performer is complex. First of all, because we cannot easily identify the aim in unequivocal terms: not all performer trainers, performers, or even spectators, will be able to agree on exactly what it is that the performer should be achieving as a product of their training. In contrast, if we were to train a sprinter, at least we could agree that the principal aim would be to be able to run as fast as possible over the distance trained for. Obviously, once this aim is established, the trainer and runner would have plenty of work to do in researching how to get to that objective. Sports science is just as complex as actor training in that sense.

Let us be aware, then, that in performer training we are often determining implicitly our aims only in the process of carrying out an exercise. Even when the actor and the actor trainer do not identify precisely the final aim of the process, the idea is there, whether we have chosen it consciously or not. This extends to all activities carried out within the context of the workshop, class, course or training studio. And that includes warm-ups.

Although the warm-up seems to be an element of training which does not impact heavily on the outcome being sought after by an extended programme of training, it will in itself assume, and lead us to accept as desirable, certain ideas about how performers and their performances function. For example, a warm-up activity that seeks to relax muscles will be assuming that such relaxation is desirable. 'But surely relaxation is always desirable?' one might object. Perhaps,

14   **THE CLOWNING WORKBOOK**

although the observation by Grotowski that his own experiments with yoga could produce detrimental outcomes for the actors' work suggests even this is a contested assumption:

> For example, we began by doing yoga directed toward absolute concentration. Is it true, we asked, that yoga can give actors the power of concentration? We observed that despite all our hopes the opposite happened. There was a certain concentration, but it was introverted. This concentration destroys all expression; it's an internal sleep, an inexpressive equilibrium: a great rest which ends all actions. [. . .] I don't attack it, but it's not for actors.
>
> GROTOWSKI 1969: 252

But the warm-up routine is not even just about physical preparedness. It also brings with it certain ideas about how we relate to a space or to each other. Exercises which ask students to move around the space such that all space is occupied, or distance is equal, induct us into an idea about space and relationships between bodies that is very precise. Such exercises, born out of the ensemble ethos which emerged in post-Second World War dance and theatre companies and practitioners, as well as music, clearly seek an outcome where the group presence often takes priority over the individual, moving as one, reacting to the unpredictable shifts of bodies, yet finding an organized, non-hierarchical and balanced whole.[1] This kind of outcome, warming up as an ensemble and producing group awareness, may not support clown learning, where relationships that foreground imbalance are regularly preferred.

In the exercises presented in this book you will find two particular ways of organizing bodies in space: the circle and the end-on audience. The circle is generally used for the initial stages of an exercise, where everyone can see, and be seen by, everyone else. Being seen and knowing one is being spectated is a key element in clown training, as we shall frequently see. The disadvantage of the circle is its symmetry. If clowns gravitate towards imbalance, then creating the habit of being in a well-balanced circle can eventually be limiting. (Then again, circles also contain their own potential imbalance, between being in the perimeter and being in the centre.) In the second configuration, 'end-on', one larger group spectates and another smaller group is spectated

INTRODUCTIONS AND WARM-UPS 15

upon. This sets up in the simplest way possible the task of the clown, to be the audience's object (of laughter).

The exercises here will hopefully carry their assumptions in full view, allowing users to make choices about how to use them. They are never 'just an exercise'. Personally, I find this particularly apposite in the field of clowning, it being a genre through which we generally question received conventions. Clowning can be a highly useful methodology in itself to explore and learn how to spot and unpick that which presents itself as the status quo and which professes not to need any justification or analysis.

1.1 Names and naming

My own questions about clown warm-ups was sparked by a disappointment with how many warm-up activities seemed to be designed to screen out the feelings present in first encounters with a group, especially the very first one, the beginning of a new course when hardly anyone knows each other or a one-off short workshop where a group come together for a brief spell, an hour or a few hours, and then depart to go back to their familiar surroundings and people. This situation is already one of 'not knowing', which is ideal for clowning, if we accept that clowns are figures which exhibit a paucity of knowledge, i.e. they are 'stupid'. Not knowing someone's name when you meet them, or then forgetting it immediately after being introduced, are social situations which most of us will have ample experience of, and the potential feelings (the negative ones) will be easily accessible. The fear of being the centre of attention for getting something wrong will likely be heightened in these first moments of an actual workshop. This is an opportunity to take advantage of, to begin the clown learning process immediately, while the building of group dynamics useful for going further into the work will get done almost without anyone noticing.[2]

The following therefore works best when a group do not all know each other, but it can also be used for a group with experience of each other previously, where the later phases of the exercise can give results just as with a new group.

1.1.1 Say your name

All form a circle, standing

- Each person says their name, going around the circle one by one. This can be repeated a couple of times.

1.1.2 Say other's name

- Say the name of the person next to you (for example, to your right).
- That person then says the name of the next person to their right, and so on, all around the circle.

Teaching tips:

- If there is any laughter, bring this to everyone's attention: laughter will be the sign that, perhaps, clowning has just occurred. This will indicate some success has already been achieved. There may even be laughter in the 'say your own name' phase, and quite possibly in the following phase, when people may forget names, or have misheard.
- Stipulate that the occurrence of laughter, being deemed a 'success', will remove the need for the person to get the other's name right.
- Now there will be two options to 'get it right': 1. Get the person's name right, or 2. Laughter.
- Now go around the circle saying someone else's name, but this time it's the person who is two people away from you. Person A says person C's name, then person B says person D's name, and so on.
- There are now more obstacles to getting it right, as often, upon hearing your name, you will assume it's your turn to name someone, but in fact it's the person before you, as we are skipping a person in the act of naming.

INTRODUCTIONS AND WARM-UPS

17

- Next, extend the gap between the namer and the named, each time around the circle getting wider. If fun is being had, this can go on until the gap is the whole circle.

Observations and feedback: ask everyone what they noticed. The most useful answers at this stage address things that we can observe objectively, such as 'lots of people laughed when they couldn't remember a name', or 'person X got it right/wrong every time'. Avoid subjective interpretations or generalized judgements, such as 'person Y is naturally funny/not funny'.

Also avoid, or discourage, attempts to try and analyze why something elicited laughter (or not), such as statements like 'it's funny when . . .'. Asking 'why is that funny?' doesn't take us anywhere, mostly because it won't be reproduceable anyway. At this point, we want to take a step back and observe. In a similar category are responses like 'I really liked it when X did Y . . .'. These kinds of observations are value judgements and may be quite common for some students to make if they have experience of more formal processes of giving constructive feedback.[3] In the clown classroom, they won't be very helpful, as they may lead us away from a cold, hard evaluation of what has happened and what the response of others has been.

Here are some examples of more useful observations for this stage:

- Person X always said 'um' before saying a name.
- Person Y got it right nearly always.
- Person Z had their mouth open all the time.
- Someone was quick in answering but usually wrong.
- X didn't look at Y.
- They pointed.

What strategies did people use when they felt they were failing or about to?

- Go silent.
- Help each other.

I ask here: which is more fun for you, to help or to be helped? Which gives rise to more jollity? Choose that option, clearly. We are not here to be polite!

Now, more specifically, ask everyone what people did when they were having problems naming somebody correctly. Usual answers may be:

- making up a name
- shouting
- blushing
- they breathed fast
- X pulled their clothing
- Y kept saying names
- Z was silent.

And: What strategies would you use in normal life when you feel you are failing to name someone properly?

- Ask the person their name.
- Apologize.

Often, these habitual social strategies won't be utilized in the classroom exercise. Why not?

Note here the nature of some of the ordinary, common mistakes that this exercise induces:

- don't know their name;
- can't remember their name;
- haven't been paying attention;
- can't follow how many places round the circle.

Notice that all these failures would fit nicely in a description of failed students in 'normal' education. These would be seen as problems to be corrected so that the student can learn properly. That probably means that they will turn out to be advantages in learning clowning. Actually, one of the great advantages that can happen with this exercise is when

INTRODUCTIONS AND WARM-UPS

someone arrives a little late for the start of the class and we are already doing the exercise. If this happens, the late-comer can be happily greeted by congratulating them on being at the advantage of relative ignorance. For, as they don't know the instructions or rules of the exercise, they are more likely to get things wrong, get laughed at and be perceived as a clown.

1.1.3 Name until we laugh

- One person now says everyone's name, only stopping once they have either named everyone in the circle, or when there is laughter.
- Each person does this in turn.

Teaching tips:

- Most people will do this going around the circle in turn, naming each person in order. Some, however, may choose people randomly around the circle. Don't discourage this.
- There is no reason for such unspoken rules of symmetry to be followed in clown training. In fact, symmetry may work against our aims. It is best to allow and encourage any variations or the 'breaking' of unspoken rules. If we want certain behaviour to be engaged in, then let us state that. The rule is, then: if a way of doing things hasn't been explicitly forbidden, then it is understood to be permitted. No unspoken rules!
- Also, at some stage, it is worth asking the question 'what did you feel when you were getting it wrong?' Common answers might be: embarrassed, stressed, anxious, tense, stupid. These are all feelings we experience in moments of social failure, and they will all be of great use later, so it's worth pointing them out early on.

By this point, we have most probably been experiencing some moments of clowning already. And we will be introduced to some landmarks, such as the presence of laughter, the feelings of failure, and an eye for observation without judgement.

1.2 Wrong naming

- One person is asked to name everyone again, but now they must give each person the wrong name. Use all the names in the room once (unless there are duplicates), simply switching them around.
- Continue until you have wrongly named everyone, or until there is laughter.
- Each person does the same.

Remember there are two ways to succeed: get it right, or provoke laughter. Your turn is over when we laugh. That means it's up to the next person to grab their turn as soon as the previous person has provoked laughter. Don't wait around for permission.

1.2.1 Wrong naming in teams

- Now go round the circle wrong-naming people again, but this time the task is performed by two people (standing next to each other in the circle).
- Then do the same with teams of three people doing the wrong-naming task.

Teaching tips:

- When describing the task, give an instruction which doesn't suggest too much in which way the participants do the task. For example, a good instruction could be 'as a team of two, give everyone the wrong name'. Or 'do the job together'.

Observations and feedback:

- After everyone has done the task or, if you prefer, after each team, ask everyone what they observed.
- How did each pair interpret the instruction?

INTRODUCTIONS AND WARM-UPS

- What was their strategy?
- What relationship could we see emerge from their efforts?

Some outcomes will feel productive for clowning and others not so. A strategy which many employ in a workshop situation is to try and voice the names simultaneously, speaking at the same time as their partner. Unless there occur some serious problems for the two to coordinate, this approach will be unlikely to produce clowning. If, as sometimes happens, the whole group take this path, repeat the exercise but with this tactic prohibited.

Likewise, there may be a tendency to 'take turns' in a pair, such that one person says a name, then the other says the next one and so on. If this happens, ask why? The answers might be of the type;

- to work together;
- to be fair;
- to be polite.

If you press this questioning still further, with 'why did you want to be fair/polite/together?' the answers may lead to realizations that this is what is expected in other kinds of performance training. In some improvisation training, for example, the concern with 'accepting all offers' may lead, perhaps erroneously, to a kind of yes-saying which erases conflict, tension or spark between performers. In the wrong hands, this philosophy can lead to a preference for the bland, the overly agreeable which can even be interpreted as a grandiloquent manifestation of 'democracy'.[4]

Clowns don't have to worry too much about democracy, happily. Undoubtedly we have to work together respectfully. But the drive for clowning will come from inequality, gross misrepresentations, extreme contrasts, and just about everything that we consider the 'worst' about ourselves. Its philosophy may have more in common with a medieval aesthetic of the grotesque, than a liberal, enlightenment one. This clown functions to degrade the noble.[5]

In this approach, debasement and mockery act on the material level, the living and dying body, which itself becomes the joke. Degradation becomes celebratory. This is far from the logical rule-bound systems of enlightenment thinking.

Let us consider the difference between a theatre class and real life. I can't imagine a real-life situation where I and a friend take turns to introduce people. We would find a way to do the task together. This means finding two complementary roles in the same task. The roles could help or hinder each other, but they won't be identical.

What fun relationships can emerge?

- One decides all and the other speaks the names.
- One decides and speaks all, the other waits, miserably, or happily, or admiringly.
- One points, one speaks.
- One asks the other, who replies, the other obeys, or does not!
- One looks at the other, the other at the named person.
- One corrects the other.
- One is agitated, one is calm.
- Both have a discussion and argue about who is who, one coming out on top.

Next, the same in trios. Here the principle is similar, it will be the relationships which make us laugh, but the possibilities are more complex. Some fun three-way relationships might be:

- Two agree, one is left out.
- One decides, another executes, third disagrees.
- One tries to decide but is overridden by second, third backs up second.

What many of the trio relationships have in common is that there may emerge first a duo, along the lines of the previous pairs, then the third must find their role as an outsider. This outsider could be helpful, accepted, rejected, disruptive, engaged, disengaged. All of these are ways of being in relation to the others. The emergence of trios often recalls the classic trios of circus clowning, the whiteface, the counter-auguste and the auguste, where the two enter into a dramatic relationship, with conflicting roles, the third being in another world, or unable to enter their world.

INTRODUCTIONS AND WARM-UPS

So we can see that politeness is not the best way to produce clown relationships. Or, indeed, theatre in general!

How long is it before we laugh? It doesn't matter. Some clowns get a quick laugh, some a late one. In this exercise, when there is laughter, you can say, next person's turn. Or let it run. Both ways allow for learning. The latter gives more practice, the former emphasizes the lesson that there are two ways to succeed for a clown: get it right, or get a laugh. Ultimately this is the more important lesson.

Should I try to be wrong/funny?

Deliberately being wrong is something a lot of clown teachers, students or performers would flinch in horror from. Firstly, this general disapproval may be a good reason for going down that path of contradiction. Anything that doesn't have broad agreement is possibly a good clown strategy, and that includes rebelling against the clowns' own orthodox beliefs. It may be perceived as being inauthentic, in an age where many believe that clowning is an expression of authenticity.

But let's also consider it from the point of view of the mechanics of laughter. Observe, when someone deliberately names someone wrong, did we laugh? In some cases we do, in others we don't. The deliberate falsehood may provoke laughter (in which case, it's a good thing surely?) or it may not (in which case it may be a flop, of which more later on). The measure here will be the laughter response, not the intention.

It may happen that some students, on hearing the instruction 'name incorrectly', despite the warning to use only the names in the room, will say other names, of persons not present, or they will make names up, or just repeat one name many times. There's nothing wrong with rebelling against the teacher's instructions in this way. But then observe the results of this 'creative' approach. Did we laugh, or not? Were their attempts to be creatively funny actually funny? Were they excruciatingly awful? And then, consequently, ridiculously funny? Were they funny because they failed to be funny? If you tend to fly off into fantasy worlds, at least take the time to observe your audience: did they laugh? Otherwise your creativity will merely be serving yourself.

Clown principles

Already, in this simple, seemingly ordinary process of learning and then messing around with our names, we are discovering some fundamental principles which seem to make clowning happen. We had already seen how success can be achieved by two routes (actual success, or laughter). Now we can see that when there are two or three people in action, they start to become clown-like when we witness their relationships. And when those relationships provoke laughter.

It is well worth initiating a brief discussion on what could be the factors in how relationships elicit our laughter.

- What appears to be ridiculous in a relationship?
- Is it when it dysfunctions?
- Or when it functions well but in an unequal way?
- Is disagreement productive for clowning?
- Or not?

In a sense, this first exercise is like an accelerated microcosm of a whole course, when you are confronted with a situation full of unknowns and small obstacles to saving face in front of your peers, whether they be familiar or strangers to you until a few minutes ago.

- How do you respond to the others?
- How do you feel about how you respond?
- Who are these other people?
- How am I relating to this one, or to this group?

The beginnings of groups of people coming together (for a workshop, a course, or any kind of group event) can reveal a whole bundle of hopes, fears, anxieties and excitement. All of these sensations are extremely useful for clowning. So it's worth taking advantage of them right from the start, when they are raw and quite obvious to you. Those raw feelings are often what warm-ups or introductions are designed to palliate. We want to feel at ease and comfortable, without anxiety. And only after getting to that comfort do we think we will then start to do the 'real' work. But in clowning we might reverse this process. Our source will often be the uncomfortable, the awkward. In any case, playing openly with these kinds of social *faux pas* (forgetting someone's name and so on) will not, hopefully, augment anxiety but instead make us feel

INTRODUCTIONS AND WARM-UPS

at ease with ourselves. It becomes a silly game, played with what we fear. Suddenly, everything feels a lot easier.[6]

You start to learn stuff about your classmates, or at least you might think you do. This one likes to win, this one appears passive but look, they are actually playing with the one who thinks they're in charge, by not doing what one thinks the other should be doing, but they can't work out how the other is resisting, but we onlookers can see it as clear as day.

This 'warm-up' can even be taken as a crash course in clowning in ten minutes. (You may wish to stop reading this book here. And why not?)

CASE STUDY 1.1

Clown workshop at AFDA, Johannesburg, April 2018

This group, made up of students of AFDA and more experienced professional performers from the improv and stand-up scene in Johannesburg, demonstrated a particularly detailed and thoughtful approach to observations and feedback on exercises, including the naming, on the first morning of a five-day workshop.

Jon Did you notice what your body did when you got things wrong?

Student I was swaying.

Jon Do you remember? A lot of people were reaching. You had one hand on your head and one here.

Student Kind of 'I need to pee' position.

Jon I hadn't asked you to observe that so you may not remember. Did you? I'll ask you a lot of times to observe what you do. If you say I was failing, that's an interpretation.

What did they do?

Student She was asking, as if they knew their own wrong name. when she finished she did this . . . [demonstrates a gesture]. It looked strenuous.

26 **THE CLOWNING WORKBOOK**

Jon What kind of tension?

Student In the neck. You had this tension, but then you had that ah and release with the smile.

Jon Both good things for clowning. Certain tension and certain relaxation. And they started to argue about it, there was an intervention.

Remember what they did.

Student They used agreement. They were eager to agree.

Jon How did they agree?

These two said it at the same time, though one would stand like this, in charge, in both teams.

Jon Who was who, when?

The tension in each person, was the one in charge more anxious? Or the one agreeing.

Student These two mirrored each other.

Jon All these things you've done are choices you made, they could have been different.

What happened here?

Student They're a team.

Jon In which way?

Student They started close to each other. Then as they got their relation, they separated. The whispering, an aside, then together. When they messed it up, it was amusing.

Jon Remember, recall, moments when we laughed the most.

Jon After all that effort, this little thing happened, an anti-climax.

INTRODUCTIONS AND WARM-UPS

[NB the teams here are not amazing or incredibly funny but their observations are good. Are they good because it's like analyzing characters, or directing actors?]

Jon What do we know about these two?

Student They both want to be team players.

I thought it would make me nervous.

They seem insecure, their body language is now you, now me.

Jon One way to understand a clown is insecurity, for us and our enjoyment.

Student I didn't know who they looked at.

I have a tendency to be very bossy.

Jon So maybe you're funnier when you're bossy.

Be bossy. Now it gets done, if you just say yes, and she decides. Isn't that what happens when you're nervous, you let someone else do it. Is it fun to not respond when someone asks me to act?

Next team?

Student They whisper a lot. Have a plan.

Jon When did we laugh most?

Student When they argue.

Jon Three big laugh points. 1 in the pre-discussion. 2 when said same name. 3 after finishing. We can find people ridiculous before, during and after.

Student They got it wrong, then they had an argument about it!

Both bossy.

Jon What kind of relationship is two bosses?

Jon Is one in charge, do they like each other?

Next.

Student They try and fake a conflict. It isn't funny.

Jon When was the moment of fun?

Student When he said, you lead. It was a moment of honesty. Saying or doing what's on our spectator minds.

Jon The clown is our representative in the show.

Student I saw anticipation.

Jon When?

Student One wanted the other to do something, the other refuses.

Jon Is that good? Is it funny? depends, if we find it ridiculous. What is clowning? Not a particular thing, but whenever we find it ridiculous. It wasn't funny, when they tried to be funny.

We're going to see this a lot. Because we know clowns are funny, so we will try to be funny. Sometimes it will be. Or not. What counts is the result. You can try to win the world cup, but who knows? Oops, wrong comparison.

You might hear, don't try to be funny, but it doesn't actually matter. We'll come to that.

CASE STUDY 1.2

Clowning and Puppetry workshop, London, April 2019

This was a one-day workshop for a mixed group of participants interested in either clown, puppetry or both, with a divergent range of experience levels. Most of the work was with objects and puppets but the starting point needed to be the basics of clowning principles. The naming game served as a practical immersion into a number of key elements of clowning which would serve as guides throughout the rest of the work. Only one other clown exercise would be needed (Step-Laugh, see later).

INTRODUCTIONS AND WARM-UPS

There are schools of thought that hold that clowning is a complex art which requires maturity, self-awareness and time to assimilate, and thereby cannot, or should not, be taught in a short space of time. Nor should it be expected to be suitable until one has undergone training in less challenging aspects of performance. However, the use of exercises based on laughter response do seem to function perfectly well in such contexts, being amply usable by the inexperienced or in very short timescales.

Figure 1 That Was Funny: Athena Amoret, Kaisa Koskinen, Jum Faruq.

2
NAME TAG

This is a commonly used game these days, in clown training and beyond, and goes under various names according to who you learn it from first. It's a good exercise to go onto immediately after the naming exercise, a more physically active way to play with the newly learned names. It evolves from being a basic children's game with fixed rules, to an exercise designed to train specific skills and ways of being in front of an audience together with other clown performers. I have written elsewhere about using this game (*Clown Training – A Practical Guide* 2015: 33), but here I give more detailed ways to evolve from the game to clowning via laughter response.

2.1 Name Tag as a game

- One person starts by trying to tag someone else; if you get tagged, you are out of the game; but if, before getting tagged, you say the name of someone else who is in the game, you are saved and the named person is now on it.

- The game ends when there are only two people left.

There are many ways to get this wrong and so be out, for example:

- Fail to say someone's name.
- Say the name too late.
- Say the tagger's name.
- Say the name of someone who is already out of the game.
- Say the name of someone who isn't in the room.
- Say your own name.

- Say a name when you hear your name, instead of chasing someone.

Option: depending on how much time you want to spend with this, now have a small group (five is a good number) play the game while the rest watch and observe, perhaps giving each player more than one 'life'. Have everyone take a turn in at least one reduced group while the others watch.

After playing the game in its basic form as many times as you like, now start to introduce some new instructions.

2.1.1 Strategies

Use a definite strategy to play the game. Come up with one way of trying to win and stick to it throughout the game. Some fun and common strategies are:

- Run as fast as possible.
- Stay in one place and assess who is where.
- Stay behind one person and wait to hear your name to surprise-tag them.
- Hide somewhere so that people forget about you.
- Push someone else near to the person who is on it.

Teaching tip: some clown training emphasizes the making of decisions in the present moment, but clowning does make good use of planning. Of course, our plans do not always have success. And that is when we might be a clown. Encourage ludicrous as well as sensible strategies.

Option: now have small groups being watched play the game with the new instruction.

2.1.2 Play for excitement, not to win

There are some games that can be played again and again, and boredom never seems to set in. Then again, it depends on the person, and on the game. Erosion of pleasure through repetition is a natural process. In line with this, now ask the players to play not with the aim of winning at all costs in the forefront of their minds, but instead with the priority of augmenting the excitement. Play it so that you get the maximum pleasure out of it, which might mean either the chaser or the chased get their pleasure heightened. Or any onlookers. Don't tag unless it's fun.

Some common tactics to augment pleasure and excitement (both one's own and that of others) are:

- Delay tagging someone who cannot escape to increase their reaction.
- Put yourself at risk of losing.
- Try to tempt others to come closer, rather than pursuing them.
- Change rhythm suddenly, from cool and calm to explosive and noisy.
- Scare or surprise each other.

Teaching tip: point out that the rules of the game remain the same, but that the players' focus is slightly shifted. Think of when you play a game with someone much younger than you, and take pleasure in the fun, rather than beating your younger sibling every time. (Though that is also fun.) It may be that some players find it difficult to make this switch, perhaps because they derive great pleasure from being competitive. Note and observe this, neutrally. It may be a key to these players' drives and hence important in finding out how they will make themselves look like fools (clowns). Others may prefer to play for fun than to win. An extreme case of playing for fun vs. to win is the player who chooses to get themselves out, perhaps because they have a lot of fun losing or because they just don't like this game! All these choices will be useful for clowning.

Option: now have small groups being watched playing the game with the new instruction.

2.1.3 Don't go backwards

The new instruction is now to make sure you never move backwards. No 'in reverse' running or walking. You may turn around and move in another direction, but always with one foot in front of the other.

Teaching tip: each new instruction in the series of exercises is your new conscious concern, rendering previous instructions semi-automatic. It's like driving while thinking or conversing or thinking about the shopping. Or any job giving you space to do other things at the same time. Emphasise the task of focusing on the newest instruction whilst letting the rest take care of itself.

Option: now have small groups being watched play the game with the new instruction.

Observations and feedback: ask those spectating how well the players stuck to the newest task of not going back. If they didn't, then what were they thinking about? Winning? Something else?

What did the instruction to move forwards do to you? What did your walking/running feel like or look like?

Moving forwards when afraid (of being tagged and losing the game) is counter-intuitive, obviously. The instruction will put you at risk more. How do you respond? Is it more interesting to see someone in more critical moments, or someone who is expert at avoiding them? Or both?

Several physical outcomes:

- You look funny trying to make yourself go forward.
- You face forwards and look for action to happen.
- You get confused and make errors and look stupid.

My own most frequent observation, and the one I find most useful to build on, is that often a person appears not just simply to be walking or running, but to be 'doing walking'. By this I mean to suggest that the action, of walking, is being 'performed'. The effort involved in making oneself walk forwards seems, by introducing a new conscious awareness of your habitual way of moving, to distance yourself from that simple action. It puts your action in quotes, as it were. It feels like 'pretending to walk (run)'. The notion of pretending is, obviously, at the root of acting, and it will serve us well in an exploration of the relationship between the performer and the clowning that they perform. Further, I would say that 'pretending' is a much more useful term than 'playing', which is a very broad term with multiple connotations, yet remains fairly vague and non-rigorous. More of this later.

Pretending is easier to understand at the level of more complex tasks for the actor, such as 'pretending to be Hamlet', or 'pretending to be dying', or 'pretending to be feeling jealous'. But physical actions are also 'pretendable': 'I am pretending to walk.'

Throughout the history of actor training there are many examples of attempts to identify the relationship between the actor and their actions, obviously not all in the same way, but parallels are frequent across seemingly disparate systems. See, for example, Stanislavski's 'I am being'.[1] Or the same idea from Gaulier, arch critic of Stanislavski.[2]

2.1.4 Play for an audience

The next new instruction is done with the small group of five or so players playing while the others watch. The players must now look at the spectators around 50% of the time. It doesn't matter in which moments, but overall the task is to split your attention between the game and the onlookers. And remember, all previous instructions still hold: play for fun, don't move backwards.

Observations and feedback: roughly how well did the players do in splitting their attention 50/50? If they looked at us only 5%, for example, why was that? Some common answers to this are:

- If I looked at the spectators, I was afraid I would lose.
- I forgot.
- I was looking at who was on it.
- I was thinking what to do.

These responses normally suggest that letting go of winning hasn't yet been attained. This is quite normal at this early stage. However, it is worth insisting on the possibility of changing one's conscious focus. After all, we are under no obligation to play to win or play the game 'well'. Ask yourself, what would happen if we were really rubbish at a game? We would be laughed at and feel embarrassed or ashamed? Perhaps.

Some players at this stage may already be discovering that they take pleasure from attending to the audience whilst being in the midst of this silly game that they don't really care about. Some others may take this step much later. But eventually we shall all hope to let go of the game and its rules and instead find the joy of playing for others. In fact, attention to the rule-bound game will never be likely to produce any actual clowning. It will more probably be the distancing from being bound by those rules which gives us the clown.

2.2 Laughter response

The next instruction takes us into a different kind of dynamic relationship between players and spectators and is a key step on the route from rule-based games to non-ruled clown performance.

In small groups (five works, but then reduce the group to three performers), play the game (with all the instructions so far accumulated, and with each person playing having two or three lives in order to spend a little stage time), but with the added rule:

- No-one can be out if there is laughter in the room.

Or, to put it more poetically:

- No lives may be lost when there is laughter.

This means, for example:

- If you are on it and are about to tag someone, but hear laughter, your tagging would have no effect, so it is pointless doing it.
- Conversely, if you are in danger of being tagged and losing a life, you might do something to provoke laughter and thereby save yourself.

NAME TAG

- If you make a common mistake, like saying your own name, that provokes laughter, you are saved.

In general, allow a few seconds after an event to judge whether or not there is any laughter that might save the people involved.

Once this version has been done a few times, it will start to become clearer that there are now a variety of ways to 'save yourself':

1 Turn and run.
2 Say a name.
3 Be funny.

Given that now you have an escape route which is in the hands of the audience, building on this, further explicit instructions can be added. When you feel in danger of losing a life:

- Look at the audience (in case they are about to laugh).
- Move forwards and towards the audience.

As noted previously, moving forwards is counter-intuitive in situations of 'danger'. But with the option of laughter as your saviour, it becomes perfectly logical to move towards the audience, either physically or only by means of eye contact. In some cases, it feels like running to the audience crying for help!

Observations and feedback:

- How much did the players notice the laughter?
- Did they respond to it?
- Were they able to manipulate it?
- Were their attempts to provoke it successful?
- Failures?
- Or failures that then made us laugh because they were such flops?
- How did the new concern with the audience's response affect how people played?

At this stage, some students might be perceiving the potential change brought about by this realigning to the audience's laughter response. Once your attention is drawn by this kind of conversation with the audience, how are your performance choices changing?

If, for example, you discover that the audience laughs when you offer yourself up to be tagged, then it will surely be an obvious next step to keep doing this. This is vastly different to the first stages of playing the Name Tag game, where there would be no perceptible advantage in sacrificing yourself as a loser. But now being a loser has a recompense. This is one way of understanding how playing to the rules of a game does not in itself produce clowning. What could produce clowning is, as we can now begin to see, a particular way of attending to the audience and to their response of laughter, or indeed its absence.

2.3 Forgetting about the game

Now that you begin to feel comfortable with the dynamic conversation you are engaging in with the audience, where your choices become determined by that engagement, you may realize that sticking to either the explicit rules of the game, or the implied habitual 'rules' of how we think it should be played, is not obligatory. This realization may in turn lead to a feeling that you are free to do what you want. And, of course, you are. So now you don't have to do actions to win the game, and you can move towards someone even if you're not on it. The rules still exist but you don't have to use them if it doesn't suit you.

This gives us a new version:

- A group of three can do anything they want. If there is laughter, the actions can continue. If not, someone must lose a life, or leave.

This keeps the final format we reached, the dynamic conversation with the audience, but dispenses with the children's game we began with.

This is an advanced step to take, so it may not be appropriate for everyone at this stage. If not, then come back to it later on. The choice about when to use exercises, for how long and to what level of difficulty, will always be one that the teacher or participants will have to make in the moment, depending on the current mood, energy levels and clarity of understanding which is apparent in the group. Don't expect all groups to respond alike. Nor should you expect the same exercise to function in the same way in all cases. I have used this final, supposedly difficult phase, described just now, as a stand-alone way of getting swiftly to 'advanced' clowning with a group that just 'got it' immediately.

This shift can be characterized as a move away from 'finite games' and towards 'infinite play'. Abandoning the obligatory nature of rules does not mean that there is nothing 'at stake'. But it does mean that you will not depend exclusively on having so-called 'high stakes'.[3]

CASE STUDY 2.1

Clown workshop for dancers, London, June 2017

When asked to lead a group studying dance performance, this exercise served to open up some new approaches to movement.

For those interested in studying movement, try and concentrate on getting to the key points described earlier that relate to:

- approaching and distancing (chasing, running away);
- strategies designed around concepts of space (stay in centre, hide at edges, move constantly);
- modulating the basic movements through attention to levels of excitement;
- observation of eye-contact and focus on each other and spectators;
- effects of prohibition to walk backwards;
- modulating impulses by attention to laughter.

The interest here is not to change the exercise radically, but to adapt it to the priorities determined by the genre or mode of performance, in this case dance/movement. Many clown exercises can be adapted in such a way, even those parts which deal explicitly with laughter.

CASE STUDY 2.2

Clown workshop at AFDA, Johannesburg, April 2018

Here as in the previous section is a transcript of some of the conversations, feedback and observations reflecting on this exercise.

Jon What happened?

Student You forget your own name.

Jon How do you know that he was panicking?

Student The screaming, running.

I love the outrage, when you lose from someone next to you.

I spent most of the second game trying to hide.

Jon Any other strategies?

Student You forget you have a way out.

Jon Did you always get the person out as soon as you could?

Student No.

Jon Why not?

Student Because it was fun.

Jon If you hate the game, maybe that's funny. Don't worry if you hate something.

Student What happened in this one?

There's time to do other things. You play so much you forget the game.

Jon That's good.

Student She was lost.

Jon That's fun, we like her lost.

Student   I love their different personalities.

My strategy was to find people who weren't paying attention.

JO starts calling out names whenever she wants, people get annoyed!

Jon   What did you notice?

Student   Rules changed!

Jon   We're in the process of going between a game/sport and something which is a show. We have a couple of steps more to get to clowning. We're kind of spoiling the game a bit now in the transition period.

Student   It was unfair.

Jon   Another good definition of clowning. That's probably what's nice about you, we love it when you feel it's always you who is targeted.

Why do we do what we do? As clowns, so that people will be entertained.

Jon   JE was funny, she hadn't slept.

Student   Sometimes being sleep deprived can put you in an unguarded state, which is fun. That doesn't mean you have to suffer to be an artist. All I mean is to say you don't have to be at your best to clown, you can be in a bad state and still clown.

LI disappeared behind the curtain, then appeared telling herself how to walk [forwards]. And M., too. Walking forwards is a bit like the voice putting you into flop problem zone. Same as walking forwards. We only walk backwards to avoid something dangerous. Forwards puts you in things, where things will happen and we can laugh at you. As well: telling yourself to do this looks like you are 'pretending to walk'. Lisa: she's walking but she's telling herself to walk. She is walking but it's also a performance of walking.

So clowns pretend things, I can pretend to be Russian or Macbeth. But also I can pretend to do physical things, like walking. If you think of clowning like that, everything is a pretence.

Can LI reproduce it?

CASE STUDY 2.3

Undergraduate Physical Theatre students, University of Stellenbosch, South Africa, March 2018

This group took particular delight in not being able to move backwards. So much so, that they came up with a new name for it: 'no *backsies*'. This clarity made it easier to reflect on the effects of the *'backsy'*.

CASE STUDY 2.4

BA European Theatre Arts students and graduates, Rose Bruford College, London, September 2017

This was a group of around a dozen current and recently graduated students from the BA ETA, which is a course that explores the broad range of theatre practices beyond the mainstream UK theatre scene. There is a strong ensemble and physical/visual performance aspect to the course.

Jon   We'll play a game, then we'll destroy it to make it work for clowning.

Student   Same three names were heard more than others.

I like it when you say your own name.

Jon   What movements did people make? Can you describe? Or do you have to demonstrate?

[JA demonstrates, imitates a move back, trying to stay on the spot, return to the spot but stepping back to avoid the tag.]

Jon   So at the moment we're playing it as a sport.

Student   The game as sport can be fun to watch, people's facial expressions, mistakes, engagement. But it doesn't really amount to a spectator event. Or sport. Most sports even don't just rely on the excitement of the game. They involve an engagement with the teams, either because it's your home town or because you bet money on them.

The threat element was enough to activate me. That physicality. When you face someone, oh what's going to happen?

Jon It might not be that aggressive scary thing, it might be something softer, when you look someone in the eye, what's going to happen, what are you going to do? The relationship. That's what's interesting about the performer relationship.

Student The game sets you up to be afraid.

Jon The process then takes you into other strategies for dealing with fear: approach, audience laugh . . .

Jon Taking yourself out of the instant tension of the game, gives you a distance from your actions, feelings, physicality.

Student I realized I distrusted people near me in case they got their name called.

Jon But if you want to augment our excitement, you might put yourself in that position where you distrust others.

[Observations of groups playing with the 'don't move backwards' instruction.]

Jon Part of you says I'll do this, but then the conscious decision says something else, leaving you unbalanced. Habit vs. decision, when they go against each other, it's interesting, or funny. What happens to your body in movement, when the mistake is to 'behave habitually', in terms of my instructions to move forward?

Jon Although the game is competitive, that group became a chorus advancing, an ensemble piece of play, using group power.

Student I saw personalities. RY energetic, constantly moving. Contrast with the others just jogging behind him, he was sprinting top speed.

GE chose not to catch someone, looked like she imitated them, because it's more fun than winning. Oh, I like this, this is pleasurable, this is fun.

Jon That's what I meant by maximizing the pleasure. There are options:

1 Toy with your victim, make them jump a lot, make them wait.
2 Put yourself at risk, go too close, etc.
3 Do other unnecessary stuff because you have time and space.
4 Do a different game.

Student SP had his own game, running for himself, I liked that.

JA leaning on back wall, it became a thing he did.

RO got caught in the corner about ten times!

Huge changes of tempo. Hilarious. Stops.

Jon So your instincts as performers start to engage, creating changes, surprises, let's stand behind him, let's wait, let's do something different, let's go off on my own and create gaps, and see how others respond. Will they carry on over there or will they chase me? Will I join them or not? Do I have more fun doing X or Y? I'm not telling you how to play it, except for the backwards instruction.

When you're free from the obligation to win, you can do what you want, play another game.

Jon Why not?

[Observations of groups playing with the 'look at the audience' instruction.]

Jon I see what she's thinking, I know what she's thinking. You have the impression you know what's she's thinking. Whether we do or not is perhaps beside the point. We don't need to construct a whole philosophy of truth and self on top of what, after all, is a set of genre performance conventions.[4]

It's interesting to play with what SP does, because he's not doing what he's expected to do in response to me.

Behaviour is tied up with what we try and make others do. Why isn't she doing X? This is the problem of improv. This is 'normality', this semblance that everything fits, everything is normal, expected. Accepted. The foundation of improv as a form of polite theatre. Clowning is impolite theatre. It's fun to try and deliberately thwart others' expectations about you. That's a good 'task' as a clown. Make them think you're going to, for example, run away, then you don't.

Figure 2 That Was Funny: Bienam Perez, Jum Faruq, Giedre Degutyte.

3
BALL PLAY

I have used ball play for a long time, finding it infinitely adaptable to clown training needs. Some who have studied with me would say 'over-used'! It's such a simple action that it allows for many variations and as a means to gauge one's state of body, mind and feeling. As a teacher, it also allows for an initial assessment of the levels of energy, focus and engagement in a group.[1]

3.1 Throw and catch

- All stand in a circle and throw and catch the ball.

Observations:

- What did you notice?
- What did you/others do?

These questions might seem odd, given the simple nature of the instruction 'throw and catch the ball'. Didn't we just throw and catch the ball? Perhaps. But possibly there will have been ways of doing this task, introduced without thinking about them, added to the instruction.

Some of these 'unspoken instructions to self' might commonly be, for example:

- Wait some time once you have the ball before throwing it.
- Pretend the ball is a different weight or size or shape to what it is.
- Throw the ball in an unusual or 'interesting' way.

If any of these occur, ask yourself, 'why?' Answers might include:

- Because that's how we usually play this in other workshops.

Next, we play to the same instruction, but with something added.

3.1.1 Change direction of focus

- When you throw the ball to someone, don't look at them, but instead look at someone else.

Make sure here that you do actually look someone else in the eye, not just averting your gaze randomly.

- Return to looking at the person you throw to.
- Now the catcher looks at someone who is not the person that threw the ball to them.

Try choosing different moments to look at someone, just before, during or after you catch the ball.

Observations:

- How did these two ways of playing ball affect how you made decisions?
- What did you do?

In a sense, these two ways provide all you need in terms of decision making. They take the place, potentially, of any other attempt to be 'creative', 'interesting' or anything else you think you 'should' be.

Counteracting what we think we 'should' do is a major aim of clown training. Clowns stage, embody or enact all those kinds of behaviours held to be unruly, frowned upon, ridiculed or otherwise marginalized. As performers, we train to get used to, and comfortable with, this kind of deviant behaviour. In training there is a potential obstacle here to overcome. Much other actor training is aimed at cultivating focus. This often means

BALL PLAY 49

training ourselves to respond in the way that is thought to be correct. Ball throwing games in standard actor training often reinforce behaviour which is 'correct' such as looking at the person you are throwing to. Why should this be deemed correct, though? Well, in a simple sense, it is the best way to make sure that the catcher manages to catch what you throw at them. This presupposes that this 'success' is what you are looking for. But what if helping someone else to fail were to be more constructive in clowning? It is easy to see this as more desirable. Even so, often the habits of performer training exert such a strong pull that it proves problematic for students to break away from them. This can be particularly tricky if you've received training that prioritizes the ensemble or complicity.

Instead, we could imagine clowns not as an ensemble seeking to help each other avoid failure, but as a group of individuals trying to help each fail and, hence, be clowns.

Why eliminate the creative approaches to playing ball? The simple answer is that it is going to be easier to find clown choices if we stick to the simple physical actions rather than attempting to find something which is not in the here and now. At least for the moment.

Here are some more ways to vary your ball playing. Practise each one in isolation for a while, giving yourselves just the options on offer at any one time.

3.1.2 Ball throwing variations

- *Anticipate:* catch the ball a little earlier than you normally would. This might result in a grabbing movement. With such a move, there is no time to mess around with thinking about creativity.

- *Delay:* the opposite of the previous one. Catch the ball later than usual. But don't let it drop on the floor. You will be concentrated on the delay, and all other worries about being interesting will be put aside.

- *Anticipate or delay:* now choose either option, as and when the ball comes to you.

- *Catch after turning around:* you might anticipate the ball coming to you, and you might be wrong!

- **Catch behind back:** find ways to have the hand which catches the ball behind you.

- **Catch on floor:** when you catch the ball, one part of your body (apart from your feet) must be in contact with the floor.

- **Don't catch:** the person towards whom the ball is thrown must not catch the ball. Instead, someone beside them must catch it.

- **Miss the ball:** similar to the previous options, the person to whom it is thrown will not catch it, and instead someone else will catch it behind them.

- **Catch in other hand:** it looks like you're going to catch the ball in one hand, but then you catch it in the other.

- **Catch and throw elegantly:** this instruction often suggests a whole range of movements, tempos and spatial variations. Make sure you remain focused only on the actions of throwing or catching, and don't transform the ball throwing into some other kind of scene or fictional act.

- **Catch with an unnecessary action:** catch the ball easily, whilst at the same time doing something else which is not required for the purposes of successfully catching the ball. This could mean moving another part of your body, making a sound, speaking, etc.

- **Keep one foot off the ground:** when you catch or contact the ball, make sure one foot is off the ground.

- **Keep both feet off the ground:** when in contact with ball, be in the middle of jumping off the ground. This can include patting the ball as well as catching it.

- **Contact without regard for consequence:** make contact with the ball (catching or hitting) without thinking about what happens to it afterwards. Don't try to direct it in any particular direction or manner. Focus on the moment of contact only.

- **Inhibit your impulse:** instead of throwing the ball without thinking about it, inhibit that first impulse to throw it in a particular way, and then throw it when your next impulse comes along. This way of playing is about the thrower rather than the catcher. It probably helps to have previously reached a point

BALL PLAY

where you are throwing the ball without thinking for a long time about how to do something 'interesting'/'creative'. Searching for something 'interesting' paradoxically generally leads to the reproduction of the already seen, the cliché or the habitual response. It is also a kind of impulse inhibition, but one that won't serve us well here. On the other hand, if you are about to respond impulsively but then inhibit that, another impulse can emerge fairly swiftly and without effort. After a while, inhibit the first two impulses, then the first three, or as many as you choose. The fun lies in the mix of control and non-control, both of which are highly useful for clowning.

- **Change your mind:** this is slightly different to the impulse inhibition option, in that both the original decision (aborted) and the final decision on how to throw are both consciously controlled.

- **Catch with mouth open:** this deals with not the manner of catching/throwing but on other habituated body responses. The instruction asks you to use your conscious awareness to change what otherwise goes unperceived. You could do this with any part of the body, but having your mouth open lends itself to many useful clown consequences: looking stupid, feeling stupid, exteriorizing otherwise controlled emotions or even physical involuntary responses such as salivating.

- **Catch with eyes open:** probably most people will play throw and catch with their eyes open anyway, so this instruction asks you consciously to choose this habitual response and also to go further and open your eyes as wide as possible. Try and make this happen in the same moment that you catch the ball. And then combine it with the previous option, mouth open, with the same timing. Feel free to add sound, or a little laugh, or whatever you choose.

All of these options are simply ways of varying the actions of catching. But the action never becomes something else. The fun is in the slightly odd ways of continuing to do a simple, recognizable action. The variations are potentially endless, even when you keep out of that 'fictional' territory (pretending the ball is different to how it is).

52 THE CLOWNING WORKBOOK

It is also fun to come up with sequences of ways of playing. These more complex actions engage the mind fully, keeping it well clear of trying to be clever, creative or interesting.

3.1.3 Throw/pat/catch

- In a circle, the first person throws the ball, the next one pats it, and the third person catches it. They then start the cycle again by throwing it.
- Now do this sequence in a group of three with the others being the audience.
- Look at the audience half the time.
- Now, only look at the audience when you feel something or when you have an 'oh no!' moment. Otherwise you are not allowed to look.

Forget about doing funny tricks. Think about how to provoke your friends' fun, failure and surprise. Throw so that you help your friend be a clown. That's what clown friends are: make each other look stupid.

3.1.4 Hand switching

These sequences are also great for keeping the mind diverted from the wrong thoughts and concentrated on action, plus on your companions and/or audience.

- Throw and catch the ball in a circle.
- Catch with one hand and throw with the other.
- Now catch with one hand, pass the ball to the other, then back to the first hand, then throw with that hand (e.g. catch in LH, pass to RH, pass back to LH, throw with LH).
- Next, catch with one hand, pass to other, back to the first, back again to the second hand, then throw.
- Now do this sequence in a group of three with an audience.

BALL PLAY

Observations:

- Where do people look when playing this game?

If the answer is 'at the ball', play it again prohibiting looking at the ball except at the moment you catch it first. During all the passing from one and to another, you must look at someone in the eye.

- How well was the physical task performed?

If the answer is 'not too well', repeat the exercise with the instruction to do it as well as you can. Focus on getting the catching and passing correct.

These two instructions cultivate two important habits for clowning:

- Focus on action (trying to do the action well).
- Focus on others (looking at people, not at objects).

Consequently, this training helps to avoid:

- Focus on ideas.
- Focus on self.

CASE STUDY 3.1

Clown workshop, Ngizwe Youth Theatre, Soweto, April 2018

This was a one-day workshop for a large group of teenagers who meet every Saturday to train and rehearse. Doing clowning exercises which demand you make a fool of yourself in front of your peers with such an age group can sometimes be tricky, as many teenagers feel the intense embarrassment in this context.

When playing catching the ball, we came up with a new addition:

- When there is laughter (for example, when someone misses the ball), then everyone also applauds.

The applause not only introduced as a means of emphasizing the success implied by the laughter, but also aided in training everyone to maintain the awareness of whether laughter was present or not. I have since then used the technique with any group that feels rather too shy about looking foolish. It should not merely redirect the attention away from the negative feelings of embarrassment, but actually affirm that these feelings, experienced as negative, can be celebrated. Some actor trainers view such acts of positivity and affirmation as essential.[2]

We shall see later on how this consciousness will be of vital importance in re-conditioning ourselves according to the demands of the genre of clown.

CASE STUDY 3.2

Clown workshops for primary school teachers in service training day, Southend, UK, September 2018

Three different groups of teachers chose to do a one-hour clown workshop over the course of a day. This allowed for a fairly rapid run through three or four basic exercises: such as 'wrong' naming; Name Tag; ball throwing whilst choosing to look at the 'wrong' person; making someone else funny; only throwing when it's funny.

A number of characteristics of this very particular selection of clown 'students' leapt out over the day. One observation relevant here is the extreme shame felt by several participants at not looking at the person they are playing ball with. This then rapidly transformed into a high level of excitement and fun in taking this game to the limit of participants' emotional responses.

My conclusions here were provisionally that working with clown exercises with 'beginners' or non-performers can achieve very swift results through a recognition of the emotions in play when being asked to do something that makes you feel and look stupid in front of your peers.

CASE STUDY 3.3

Open public workshop at Victoria & Albert Museum 'Friday Late', April 2018

This three-hour evening workshop took place in one of the museum's galleries during a monthly open evening on the theme of circus. Visitors were free to walk through, around or into the workshop space and participate, watch or ignore as and when they pleased.

The workshop used ball-throwing/catching as a starting point for engagement between participants and also with non-participating onlookers (audience). Because of the nature of the space, the circular set-up for ball-throwing began by forming a relatively unified group of up to a dozen participants at a time, where their focus was inwards on themselves. After a certain time playing with some of the options described above in this section, the presence of onlookers presented itself with a new opportunity not normally available to a closed workshop group. From this context, new options could be invented, such as:

- Having played 'catch while looking at someone else', now make that 'someone else' a person who isn't in the circle, someone who is standing outside the group looking in. This can be either a person behind the people opposite you in the circle, or, perhaps more fun and interesting, someone who is behind you. The instruction then becomes: when you catch the ball, look at someone behind you.

- Now look at a person behind you (and outside the playing circle) until they return your eye contact.

- The same, but maintain eye contact until the person smiles.[3] Then continue by throwing the ball to a new player.

- Now, once they have smiled, approach them.

- This can then be extended to include approaching the contacted person with a joke prop, like a whoopee cushion, or a slapstick. It can form the basis for a training in linking the contacting of an audience with the beginning of a performance, especially in the context of passers-by, such as a street.

CASE STUDY 3.4

MA Voice Studies, RCSSD, London, May 2018[4]

The task as I saw it with this group was 'to bring a workshop in clown to a group interested in voice'. Where would their own specialism lead me and the exercises I offered? That led to:

- adaptation of exercises to address specialist interests;
- invention of new variations on exercises to explore these further;
- rejection of certain exercises as not addressing interests;
- new insights from participants and teacher emerging from a specific focus.

These conditions apply, in my experience, in each and every specialist group undertaking any aspects of clown training.[5]

It soon became apparent that some of the exercises of the early stages of clown training would easily lend themselves, with this group, to provoking, eliciting and generally experimenting with sound produced by the human voice. That sound could be produced either voluntarily or seemingly involuntarily and both outputs would be useful not only for clowning but also for voice training.

With throwing and catching the ball, the involuntary reactions produced by voices, usually by those receiving the ball in an unexpected way, were quickly picked up on and we were able to elaborate further instructions for ball playing in order to capitalize on this already existent bias towards participants observing their own, and others', voice production. We were in a kind of 'double context', one where we were expecting and looking out for laughter (as a marker of clowning) but also voicing of a variety of types (as the group was accustomed to do). The exercises proposed pulled students towards laughter, but their studies pulled them somewhere else, but at the same time.

- Throw the ball to someone with the intention of eliciting/provoking others' laughs, by means of the unexpected, in timing, direction, intensity, of the throw. (See some of the options described earlier.)

BALL PLAY

57

- Now do the same but aim to produce any kind of vocal reaction. It can be laughter or something else, a shout, a cry, a murmur, a gasp, as long as it is vocally produced and audible.

What is important here is to focus on the 'intention', which is that of producing a particular kind of response in others (who can be imagined as co-performers or spectators, it doesn't matter at this point).

Can the actor, given a task of eliciting a particular response, engage in the task? Each genre of performance may have its own desired response, which may or may not have a vocal/audible element: laughter for comedy/clown, crying/anger for melodrama, silence for tragedy, answers to questions for the English pantomime or many forms of story-telling, and so on. There's a question here about just how involuntary those responses are. How far are the audience conditioned, inducted into the correct response? How far does this contract impinge upon the outcome? That is interesting to consider, but what concerns us more here is to explore how the performer elicits the appropriate responses, assuming the genre-contract to be already agreed upon. Given that the contractual responses of the clown audience are basically laughter/non-laughter, both of which are audibly marked, and thus relatively simple to objectively identify when performing, the lessons learned by clown training can usefully be transposed to other genres whose responses can be less easy to pick up on. This is valid work for any performer, clown or not.

Next, we extended the ambit of possible ways of eliciting the desired vocal responses:

Jon Throwing the ball/catching the ball is the script. Your job as an actor is to elicit involuntary sounds/vocal reactions, of yourself and/or others. You may do it without using the ball as well, using other things other than the ball-throwing [your script] . . . you may also use voluntary voice to do that.

Student Can you say that again?

Jon No.

Group laughs.

Jon For example.

THE CLOWNING WORKBOOK

Speech can in this way be used voluntarily, in order to elicit an involuntary response (in this case, a laugh). In this way, the next stage of the exercise was established:

- While throwing and catching the ball, your intention is to elicit/provoke others' vocal responses/laughs, by means of the way you perform the actions of the script (throwing, catching) or by any other means, including vocal ones.

This immediately suggested a question: what was the difference between the vocal responses provoked by the ball-throwing, and the voicing which could now be used in order to produce the intended effect in others? The clue is in the functions: the former is involuntary, and the latter is, by dint of being 'used' for an intended aim, voluntary.

With this distinction between voluntary and involuntary vocal acts clarified, we could move on to create a further stage in the exercise, with the instruction running as follows:

- If you have an involuntary laughter response during the exercise, change it into some other vocal act.

In this way, what was originally laughter comes to serve as the energy for something else, some other kind of voice, via an intentional, voluntary modifying of the involuntary response of laughing. Gaulier's concept of pleasure, as the basis upon which different genres can be built, can help here. Working in clown, the pleasure directly manifests as stupidity and laughter. Stepping out of clown as a genre, we can convert the pleasure-that-would-be-laughter into anything we choose, whose genre is as yet unspecified. This is not strictly work on genre as such, in the style of Lecoq/Gaulier, but instead work on one of the traditional conservatoire divisions of the actor's technique: voice.

Coaching tips drawn from these sessions:

- Once the involuntary response is 'out', catch it while it's hot and cultivate it, as long as it lets you.

BALL PLAY

- If your voluntary bit of 'voice acting' doesn't elicit anything . . . fine! Give up! You did a thing and it didn't get a response. No problem. A failed piece of acting. They are called flops, technically. You can only have a flop if you try to do something right, though. You just had a good flop because you aimed to do your job as an actor by trying to provoke a vocal reaction. Flops are good. It's good to vocalize your flop.

- Once you've elicited a response, your job is done, so there's no need for any more voicing, acting or whatever. Throw the ball in order to provoke a sound. Stop when you've done your job. Otherwise you end up in a path with no end.

- Sometimes you elicit the other's vocal response by playing the aggressor, sometimes the victim.

- Sometimes by being an onlooker, doing something over there that we weren't noticing.

- Don't forget the possibilities of a word, half a word, a syllable.

- It's amoral. You will do anything for a response. Actors are amoral. Because our purpose is to elicit responses, using pretence, but the responses seem real.

Once all of these possibilities had been explored as a group in a circle, the same could be experimented with in groups of three performers with the rest as spectators. The task then is to aim to provoke the vocal responses in the spectators, not in your co-actors:

- A group of three do any actions they choose in order to provoke vocal responses in the spectators.

The JOB is the provoking of sound. Being a performer.

The METHOD is the throwing and catching, the ACTIONS. Being an actor.

There are no other options, like doing a different action, or having a different objective.

The result is a complex mixture, a play between plans and reactions, intentions and surprises.

Figure 3 On/Off: Kaisa Koskinen entering the stage.

4
DOING THINGS WHEN IT'S FUNNY

This brings us to a rather particular case of ball throwing/catching options. It's particular because it will form one of the foundations of a method which places at its centre the conditioning to the laughter response. This whole area of work began to emerge in my teaching some years ago, as a set of variations on the older exercise of 'Step-Laugh' (see later), which is a simple exercise to bring actions into line with laughter. One evening, while playing ball with a group at the beginning of one of the regular weekly classes, I thought, what will happen if we throw the ball only when it's funny? We tried, and here are the results, as they have been developed since.[1]

First, the basic exercise:

4.1 Throw the ball when it's funny

- In a circle, we throw and catch the ball, but the throwing only happens when there is laughter in the room.
- When there is no laughter, the ball is not thrown.

Teaching tips:

- Don't delay when there is laughter, just throw the ball.
- Similarly, stop throwing as soon as the laughter ceases.
- If you are concerned with your attempt to be funny, you may well miss the laughter.
- Make your primary concern the registering of laughter.

The main mistake in the early stages of this exercise is to place too much attention on attempts to provoke laughter. Not that it's wrong to 'try to be funny'. As we shall see later on, this 'trying' is in fact inherent in clowning and will prove useful. But for now, the awareness should be outwards, awaiting the sound of laughter. Whilst waiting, you may do as you please, but as soon as that signal, the laugh, occurs, you should act according to the instruction. This is pure conditioning. It builds a new habit, a link between registering laughter and an action (throwing). (Be like Pavlov's dogs, and 'salivate' when you hear the laughter!)

Conditioning is simply a way to gradually create new habits that are productive for our task, which is clowning. Certain habits of thinking, focusing, or prioritizing will help that aim and other ways of thinking will lead in the wrong directions for our objective. We will mostly be concerned with laughter throughout this book. This is the 'right' kind of thinking, as it were. Then the wrong thinking would be to be concerned with whether you are funny, good, or creative.

It may help to imagine yourself as the servant of the ball. The ball cannot throw itself, as it is an inanimate object. So it cannot in itself respond to laughter. You will therefore be the intermediary, serving the purpose of the ball, which is to be thrown when we laugh.

The task here is to do the job of connecting the laughter with the action. It doesn't matter how much laughter there is or not. The aim is NOT to elicit as much laughter as possible. The aim is to be as ACCURATE as possible in your job. Compare this with some kinds of real-life jobs that involve observation and a pre-conditioned response. For example, counting the traffic. To do the job well, one must be awake to the passing traffic at the spot ordained, and record accurately how many cars pass that corner. The aim, obviously, is not to record a high number of cars. The number is not your concern. That is data that the ministry for transport will analyze, not you. We could say that the clown, in this exercise, is someone who serves, but does not analyze. Nor do they worry. They just observe reality.

Evidently, it is irrelevant who laughs, or how. Nor is it important who you throw the ball to.

- Now turn this outwards for an audience, in a group of three performers.

DOING THINGS WHEN IT'S FUNNY

Performing note: whilst the concern is with performing the scripted action (ball throwing) at the right time, when laughter occurs, there remains space and time when there is no laughter, in which the script cannot be performed. During the non-laughter periods, you can be free to do anything. Other than the scripted ball throwing.

4.1.1 Act when it's funny

Once the principle of 'the action happens when there is laughter' has become well-established, or conditioned, and you have begun to be able to respond to laughter more or less semi-automatically with the pre-arranged script of throwing the ball, you can now move on to do the same with other kinds of actions. First, let's use some other simple ones:

- Starting in a circle, move across the circle towards the other side of the circle, whenever there is laughter.
- The same, but move anywhere in the space, in any manner you wish, whenever there is laughter.

Next, we shift back to an end-on audience watching three performers:

- Three performers can do whatever they wish, whenever there is any laughter, while being spectated by the rest of the group as an audience.
- Note that it doesn't matter where the laughter comes from: the audience, or the performers, or even from outside the class space!

Coaching tip: this stage of 'doing whatever you wish' in place of an agreed script is really just a stepping-stone to the next phase, so if you find that the requirement to come up with something feels too much to cope with, don't worry. This 'improvised content' is not by any means the simplest route towards clowning, although improvisation has come to be closely associated with clown training in recent decades. We shall see, as this training develops, how it is the 'already decided action', or

4.1.2 Perform the script only when it's funny

We now come to the main objective of this part of the exercise, which is to marry up the response of laughter to your performance. To do this, we leave aside any concern for improvisation.

- In groups of two or three, spend a moment agreeing on a simple action which you can do. The actions can be anything do-able, they don't have to be intended to be funny.
- In turn, each group performs their action when there is laughter.
- When there is no laughter, they are free to do any other actions ('off-script').

You can do a few rounds of this until everyone feels comfortable with matching up their pre-decided actions with the in-the-moment laughter response. Also notice how the obligation of performing the script and nothing but the script might force you into a corner where you appear more clownish. The plan makes you do something you feel stupid about. If, on the other hand, you can improvise the script, then you are likely to avoid things that make you feel stupid. (The way to do clown improvisation, then, would be to condition yourself to do things that make you feel stupid!)

The exercise is easier and more rewarding, the more real or possible the chosen actions are.

Use specific physical or material actions or tasks:

Simple actions or activities

- Drink water.
- Do a press-up.
- Pretend to sneeze.

DOING THINGS WHEN IT'S FUNNY

- Sweep.
- Consult a map.

These 'simple actions' are physical actions that humans often do, but which often lack narrative, backstory, intention. Their purpose or aim or intention are immediately clear to onlookers, as they seem to be achieved almost in the moment of their inception. An 'activity' is often something which you can do continuously, but which doesn't change your circumstances in any noticeable way. So you can do it for a while. Once you start thinking, there are countless ones to try out: Yawn, Sneeze, Cough, Swear, Fall over, Walk on tip-toe, Do a handstand, Jump, Pretend to sleep . . .

Simple linear tasks

Linear tasks are a series of actions which, when performed one after the other, take you from one state or situation to another. 'Simple' versions are those whose linear narrative is almost immediately apparent to onlookers. Such as:

- Put all the chairs in a stack in the corner.
- Get dressed/undressed.
- Sing a song.

Multi-role actions or tasks

When we have two or more performers, these types of script assign distinct roles to each performer, but within a common objective. The most obvious examples may resemble status-defined labour, such as:

- Task is to clear away the chairs: performer A instructs the others, performer B moves chairs to one place, performer C stacks chairs.

However, also within this simple category are the basic 'dramatic' situations we are very familiar with:

- Performer A attacks performer B, who escapes.
- Hug each other.
- A and B meet as lovers, while C interrupts.

- A scene where person A kicks person B, and person C tells A to stop.
- Person A hides person B from person C.
- This script should use all the actors in different roles, such that instead of all doing the same agreed action, each person takes a role which complements the others, but within the same overall action.

Devising scripts: in groups of two or three, spend some minutes agreeing on a simple script which you can do.

Teaching tip: it can help to understand how to build a script with different roles if you think, 'how many performers do we have?' Let's make use of them all. Let's not waste a performer doing the same as another, for which they are not needed.[2]

4.1.3 Perform a funny plan (only when it's funny)

Despite constantly insisting that planned actions don't have to be thought of as funny in themselves, leaving us space to focus on the audience reaction, it is inevitable that the desire to plan to be funny will not go away. And nor should it. At this point, there may well be more of a desire surfacing, as you attempt to perform your scripted actions, to find the way to get your shows finished in front of your audience. The desire to find the laugh may become more pressing. Earlier, we emphasized the objective observational job of the clown, in order to leave aside any anxiety about being funny. But now this desire is to be expected and welcomed back.

If you want to dive straight into trying 'funny plans', then go to Section 17 later in this book. But as a first taster, try something like this:

- In groups of two or three, spend some minutes agreeing on a simple script which you can do.
- This script should have as its main concern, the intention to make us laugh when you perform it.
- It will be enough at this stage of the training, just to have the intention to be funny. Later on, we will look in depth about

DOING THINGS WHEN IT'S FUNNY

67

strategies for achieving this. So don't worry if you feel you don't know how to achieve such a script.

There are a number of ways to manoeuvre within this situation:

- Continue to be as accurate as possible.
- When free from the obligation to do your script in response to our laughter, use the opportunity to try out all kinds of off-script actions, experiment to see what provokes our response.
- As soon the response comes, jump back on-script. Accurately.

Generally, there begin to emerge different kinds of off-script, which operate on distinct levels. As and when these occur, recognize and identify them. These are the most obvious:

- Doing something with the express intent to try and provoke laughter (whether successfully or not).
- Talking or arguing with your fellow performers about the way to perform your script.
- Expressions of how the performers feel about the performance and how it's going (often to do with how much their intended plan matches the in-the-moment outcome).

We now have a rather complex, but hopefully clearly differentiated set of levels which are going on simultaneously in a performance:

1. Script, decided in the past, or written.
2. Performance of script, determined in the moment dependent on audience laughter.
3. Trying to be funny, in order to be able to advance in the script.
4. Talking about the performance as it happens.
5. Onstage feelings.

We can summarize the options for action and response in all levels like this:

1. Action (clown) – planned or not/scripted or improvised.

68   THE CLOWNING WORKBOOK

2 Reaction (audience) – laugh or silent.

3 Reaction (clown) – programmed/conditioned – leave/stay
– continue/stop.

4 Reaction (performer) – feelings about performing.

A note on feelings – in amongst your 'stage feelings' there will be those concerns and desires to please, to be funny or creative or clever. Even if you manage to condition yourself to respond to laughter accurately, and concern yourself less with 'wrong thinking', these feelings will not disappear completely. But in this way they may appear as something that makes you look ridiculous, more likeable, rather than less due to your suffering.

This rich network may be evident as such to an audience, or it may merge in their perception. In the end, it doesn't matter. Elements from one level could migrate to another level. For example, if, on first performance, you find that your script was decidedly unfunny at some point you had hoped it would be successful, but that one of you did something off-script which got a response and thereby enabled you to continue, this off-script element might be incorporated into the on-script for the next performance. Or acknowledging how a performer's feelings about how badly, or well, something was going, might become the manner in which the script will be performed the next time.

What we have arrived at is a kind of conversation between performers and spectators, which makes use of a pre-decided set of actions, but which are played out in response not only to those spectators, but also determined by the feelings, relationships and ideas of the performers as they seek to negotiate the situation. And what is that situation? Well, it is the quintessential clown's, or actor's, situation. Faced with an audience in real time and space, you must somehow engage with them by means of a set of actions which do not occur seemingly spontaneously, as in real life, but according to a pre-set plan, a plan that was designed to have a specific effect on those spectators, the success of which is as yet unknown, as the performance takes place in the here-and-now.

The 'conversation with one's performing partner', based upon the observation of actual, rather than fictional, behaviour, is a familiar theme in some acting methods, notably Meisner's.[3] But the 'conversation with the audience' (a different kind of partner) has a longer pedigree in a range of traditional and popular performance forms, from English panto to story-telling to Shakespeare. This dialogue, in its clown version based on laughter response, also resembles dynamic dialogues in social contexts outside of the scope of theatrical performance, most obviously between adults and young children.[4]

Here, hopefully, it has become clear how the mechanics of that conversation can play out in clowning in a way in which the performer or student can grasp and reproduce in practice. The key is that the dynamics of clowning based on laughter response only demand of the performer that they observe and act, in ways which are entirely possible, non-abstract, and non-mysterious.[5]

It's important to keep practising the mechanics of these exercises, until the links become conditioned and automatic. Once that has been gained, one can come up with any number of metaphors for what's going on. One workshop group imagined this conversation as being as if the audience held the remote control which activates and deactivates the clowns.[6]

One final variation may be useful at this point:

- Perform your funny plan only when it's funny. When there is no laughter, leave the stage.

Reminder: when leaving the stage: you were asked, in the early stages of this exercise, not to think of yourself, of what you can do, of how to be funny, interesting, creative; but instead to think only of the ball, to serve it, make sure it is being thrown when there is laughter. You were the servant of the ball. In the later stages of the exercise, when you have a funny plan and attempts to be funny in the mix, do not forget that you are only USING the plan. You are only USING the off-script moments. For what? Perhaps to see what the response is? So, TAKE YOURSELF offstage when it's not funny. YOU are now the BALL. The ball is now the CLOWN, which you serve.

4.2 Stop when it's funny

Now it's time to do it all backwards!

- Start by throwing and catching the ball in a circle, throwing the ball only when there is NO laughter, and stopping the action when laughter occurs.

- Do this for an audience in groups of three.
- Do anything you wish in a group of three with an audience, ceasing the actions when there is laughter.
- Plan an action for your group and perform this for the audience only when there is no laughter. Laughter stops your planned action.
- Plan a script with differentiated roles for your group and perform it only when it's not funny.
- Plan a funny script and perform it only when it's not funny.
- Do off-script things when we laugh and return on-script when we don't.
- Leave the stage when we laugh.

Remedial strategies: occasionally, some students, or a whole group of students, respond only minimally to this version of the exercise. There may be a sense of not knowing how to cope with doing actions for a time whilst there is no laughter, feeling that something is missing. It may be that the feelings of awkwardness are not yet ready to expose themselves, that caution and habit are still strong. Who knows? But if the laughter really isn't happening to drive the ball throwing . . . or its reverse format, then try going back to a stripped down version:

- Two people throw the ball to each other in front of the audience.
- When we laugh, they stop and look at the audience.
- When the laughter subsides, they go back to their ball throwing.

This reduces the anxiety about trying to be funny, about trying to think of something funny or creative or interesting or clever to do with the ball throwing. There simply isn't any space for that. In a sense, this puts more pressure on the student, as they may feel the awkwardness more keenly. And that is the point: to isolate this feeling so that we can all see it, and then it can be acted upon. It doesn't matter if there is no laughter for a while. Be patient and wait. At some point, one of the two will have a reaction, a feeling that we can perceive, and this is most likely to make

DOING THINGS WHEN IT'S FUNNY

us laugh. From then on, things get lighter. The fact of us laughing at them (for no perceivably sensible reason) is in itself something funny, that will provoke the next laughs. For a while. Even if there are few laughs, this exercise allows student and teacher to look at what isn't there yet, and on the feelings which emerge when one is in front of an audience. It can take time to first acknowledge these feelings, and even more time to start to want to make friends with them, finally becoming comfortable with the uncomfortable.

Ask yourself: what did I feel?

What did I think?

If you are having problems conditioning your responses to match up with laughter/non-laughter, you can practise the same kind of thing but with other kinds of objective, external events, and forget about laughter for a while. Try doing a simple action (tossing a ball in one hand while paying attention to something else:

- the traffic outside;
- the voices next door;
- your dog moving;
- every time your friend says a particular word.

Or:

- As a group, all count out loud the laughs as they happen ('1 . . . 2 . . . 3 . . . etc.'). If you miss any, go back to zero. Get to 20.

Homework:

- Pay attention to laughter. Count the laughs out in the real world as you travel, work or socialize.
- Make your observations without the need to judge the laughter. You don't need to know why it's there, nor what quality it has.

Although I have mostly been referring to laughter or its absence, since observation of laughter is a more or less objective task, I also use the description 'when it's funny' as an equivalent to 'when there is laughter'.

This gets round any subjective issues or disagreements about what the meaning of 'funny' is.

And in specific work contexts, you can adapt the 'act when there is laughter' to the usual, 'real' actions expected to be done in that context.

- Do your real job when there is laughter.
- A group of BA students leaving a classroom will have to pick up their bags, shoes, clothes and leave the room, only when we laugh.
- A group of primary school teachers on a training day can come into the classroom and hand out books, tell us to be quiet, and so on, but only when it's funny.

No laughter without action.
No action without laughter.

In the end, it's just a question of resetting your priorities. Most jobs have a priority they concern themselves with and look out for. Scientists look out for particular results in an experiment, bus drivers for passengers, charity workers for potential donors. Each worker becomes attuned, conditioned to foreground what is important in their task. Clowning is just another job, then, and not a really complicated one at that!

CASE STUDY 4.1

Clowning and Puppetry workshop, London, April 2019

With this group of mixed interests in two distinct genres, we alternated exercises from each mode of performance and then tried to find common points of understanding. Having done the basic form of ball-throwing while funny, and doing anything you choose when funny for an audience, we picked up one element from the puppetry exercises already done, using wooden sticks. (Puppetry-oriented training already sparks an interest in experimenting with different places of focus – on the stick as object, as animated object, as companion to the human, as tool, as prop.)

DOING THINGS WHEN IT'S FUNNY

Bringing the animation of sticks into the 'perform when funny' exercise gave us the following:

- Three performers each have a stick, which they 'activate' when the audience laughs.
- When there is no laughter, the sticks are 'deactivated'.
- The performers can do whatever they like while there is no laughter, except activate the sticks.

Optional choices were to:

- Hide the sticks when not activated by laughter and bring them out again on cue.
- Or have them on view always, animated when we laugh.

In this version, it appears and feels like it is our laughter which is driving the activation of the sticks. It might also seem like it means 'look at us when we don't laugh, and at the sticks when we do'. One could, in puppetry terms, also call this 'animating' the object, but this is a term which brings in a whole load of other connotations and assumptions about object theatre, raising questions that do not need to concern us right now. 'Activating', on the other hand, is a non-specialist term that could mean 'animate' but could also mean 'use' in some other way, as a prop, as a tool or as itself.

Next try varying the objects:

- Instead of one stick per person, have just two or a single stick between three.
- Use other objects.
- Use puppets.

Laughter activates the performance.
Laughter drives the action.
Laughter drives the puppet.
Laughter animates the puppet.

Figure 4 On/Off: Jum Faruq entering the stage.

5
ON/OFF

The exercise which I have over the years called Ball-Clap-Hit was covered in detail elsewhere.[1] As I wrote at the time, it was one of the two main laughter-response exercises I used, together with Step-Laugh (coming up next), and both evolved from the intensive period of teaching and research I undertook at Central School of Speech and Drama as Research Fellow from 2007 onwards. They have their earlier origins in a lineage traced back to Gaulier, being elaborations, variations and tangents of simple principles found in the work of many teachers who draw on the concept and practice of *via negativa*.

But here I want to explore how the exercise can help laughter conditioning in general and extend it into using scripts and beyond. This will involve a simple version of the initial game which can then be used as a general principle. First, let's summarize the basics of the exercise:

5.1 Ball-Clap-Hit

- All in a circle, throw a ball to anyone, whoever catches it throws it to someone else.
- Emphasize that the ball shouldn't be dropped.
- If someone drops the ball, the teacher uses a rolled-up newspaper to punish them with a firm whack on the bottom or part of the body acceptable to the group.

Teaching tips: in general, when students realize what the game is about (when the punishment is introduced) the excitement and fun levels shoot up. However, take care:

THE CLOWNING WORKBOOK

- Keep it light and playful.
- This isn't about suffering.
- It's about having a playful attitude to the anxieties and fears of failing.
- The aim is to defuse the guilt or even shame commonly attached to failure and punishment.

Clearly, any signs of real triggering of trauma in any participant must be addressed immediately. In reality, this is a rare phenomenon, depending on who your participants are, and it is relatively simple to respond to. Signs of triggering of trauma will be mostly obvious from the beginning. The participant may: signal to you their negative response verbally or facially; they may leave the space; or they may avoid participation more discreetly. Simply speak to them and express clearly that they may sit this one out, either in the room watching or leaving the space, as they prefer, and they will be asked back afterwards. Leave the choice to them entirely, with no pressure, but making it clear that the exercise will continue meanwhile and that they can return at any time. In my own experience, this has occurred less than half a dozen times amongst many thousands of students over the years. The only instance it became more problematic was when an assistant tutor felt the need to police the responses on behalf of students, withdrawing themselves as a means to signal disapproval. If you are working with others who are in a position of responsibility for the group, make sure that they are aware that you are facilitating the group in full awareness of the potential effects of clown exercises.

5.1.1 Variations

Once fun has been had for a while, we can increase the difficulty, in order to give our pleasure a little boost:

- The receiver of the ball must clap their hands before catching it (failure to clap or to catch get the newspaper punishment).

ON/OFF 77

After a while of this:

- Add that the receiver must also do a little jump as well as clapping before catching the ball (any failure to jump, clap or catch gets punished).

5.1.2 Laughter as a pardon

- Continuing as previously, now if there is any (real) laughter in the room whenever a receiver makes a mistake, then that person doesn't get punished.

After a while playing like this:

- Regardless of whether the receiver makes a mistake or not, every time someone receives the ball they will be punished unless there is laughter in the room.

Teaching tips:

- Emphasize 'laughter in the room' as opposed to 'laughed at the person'. This is the beginning of a process to detach ourselves from the anxiety around whether 'I am funny' or not. Slowly we can relinquish the 'ownership' of the laughter and hence the ownership of the 'failure to be funny'. As in previous exercises, the laughter, although it must be real, can come from anyone, from those watching, those playing, the receiver themselves, or apparently provoked by something completely extraneous, some occurrence in the space that has nothing to do with the class, such as a cat wandering across the floor, or a picture falling off the wall, or the sound of a toilet flushing. The job right now is to condition ourselves to link the laughter and its absence to particular outcomes (punishment and not punishment). We are accustomed to regarding punishment as precisely that which must be 'owned'. Which is 'deserved'. That is its whole point, if we are to follow its logic. So, this distancing might feel like an absurdity. But in fact it is a simple process of converting the 'real' into the 'played'. We are now heading towards playing at punishment, playing at failure, playing at success. In the end, we won't care so much at all. Not only is that something rather healthy, it is vital for us to be able to clown confidently.

Now we will have a look at how this can form the basis for something more 'theatrical'.

5.2 Leave or stay

- At this point, you can go back to the basic game with punishment – remove the added difficulty of claps and jumps – and also now only punish when someone doesn't catch the ball.
- Next, instead of the newspaper punishment when someone doesn't catch the ball, they must leave the circle and sit down. If there is any laughter before they have reached their seat, then they come back to the circle and continue playing.

Teaching tips: depending on the group, this can go on forever without anyone ever getting to sit down. If so, you can say that the game will end once one person is out. Otherwise, if lots of people are sitting, play it until only one person is left.

5.2.1 Free actions

- Now we replace the action of catching a ball with giving each person a free choice to do any action they want to.
- There is no set order for people to 'act', just step forward into the circle and 'do something'.
- After your action, if there is laughter, you stay in the game; if there is no laughter, you get the newspaper punishment.

5.2.2 Free actions and leave or stay

- Combining the two previous variants, anyone can do any action, which if followed by no laughter they leave the circle and sit down.

So far, we have been playing this in a circle which includes the players, moving on to ejecting ex-players to some other part of the space. Initially, our performance area is just the circle and later it is a hybrid of an inclusive circle and a separated auditorium with an active performers' area and a passive spectators' area. Although, clearly, those non-playing spectators could also be laughing, and influencing the decisions of the performers.

Now let's shift entirely over to that split auditorium, with an end-on configuration that puts performers 'on a stage' and spectators 'in the seats'.

5.3 Leave when not funny

- A group of three are onstage, everyone else sits to watch.

- Anyone of the three performers can do any action (as previously in the circle version).

- Following the action, if there is laughter anywhere, they stay onstage.

- If there is no laughter, that performer exits the stage (this can be to behind a screen, or a curtain in the wings, or out of a door in the room, depending entirely on what your space is like).

- Once offstage, you can add the possibility of a performer returning to the stage, but only if their attempt is accompanied by laughter, otherwise they continue to remain offstage.

Teaching tips: at least to begin with, take plenty of time around each action so that we can all judge whether there was or wasn't laughter, and wait to do the next action until we are sure the performer has either stayed

5.3.1 Leave when not funny competition

Here is another variation in the motivation, but on the same format:

- Three performers are onstage.
- All stay downstage, or as far from whatever exit you have in your space.
- One performer must leave when there are no laughs.
- Only one can approach the exit, the others must stay in their positions.
- The first to leave the stage wins, the last to leave loses.

Performing tips:

- You must be CONCERNED with making sure the leaver doesn't make it to the exit, by provoking laughter so that they have to return.
- Your reactions and interactions are with the audience, not with the leaver.

And now for the reverse version.

5.3.2 Leave when funny

- As before, a group of three performers are onstage.
- An individual performer does any chosen action.
- If there is laughter, that person leaves the stage.
- If there is no laughter, the actions continue.
- As with the previous version, performers offstage can attempt to return, but only if that attempt is now unaccompanied by laughter.

ON/OFF 81

Teaching tips:

- In this reverse version, the instruction to make each action individual and separate may become superfluous. What often occurs is that the three performers will engage in continuous action, whilst there is no laughter, only to be interrupted by a laugh, at which point one, or more than one, will exit. Take your time to practise this.

- The feeling of continuing to do things onstage while there is no audience reaction may well feel extremely odd at this point! In reality, though, it's just that you are absolutely free to do whatever you choose onstage, without sanction. Whether then the laughter feels to you like a punishment or not is actually not so important. All you are doing is learning to be directed by the audience, while maintaining your freedom to act. If you like, think that you can do 'any old crap' onstage.

Some more tips on how to get the most out of this exercise:

- Keep doing the action until it's funny.
- Think of it as similar to 'keep doing it until it stops being funny'.
- It's NOT a case of keeping doing something that's unfunny while disregarding the reaction.
- It IS a case of doing it with an awareness of the risk, danger, that someone might laugh, but you don't know when.
- So never judge what you do, whether it's funny or not. It's just a job.

5.3.3 On/Off pairs

Once you are familiar with both these versions, now try combining them, with a pair of performers:

- Performer A will be **onstage when there is laughter** (and offstage when there is none).

- Performer B will be **offstage when there is laughter** (and onstage when there is none).

- For more clarity, and fun, add the following lines when either performer enters or exits: say 'thank you' when you enter the stage and 'sorry' when you exit.

- Don't wait for your partner to leave, just take your opportunity by responding immediately the audience response happens.

Having to say sorry and thank you makes the thing personal again (having learned to do your job). Having detached ourselves from any concerns or fears or worries about whether it is (I am) funny or not, we now reintroduce the personalization through the text. But it's a trick, a pretence, a staging. So it might be funny now that it looks like the clown thinks we're laughing because they are so good.

5.4 On/Off with scripts

This exercise began with a limited action (throw and catch the ball) which was an instruction given by the teacher to the students. It was a kind of script. It told the players what to do and precluded any alternative actions that may have been invented by the players. Obviously, it didn't tell the player 'how' they should throw or catch, just that this is what they should do. Equally, of course, anyone could at any time have decided to do what they wanted (we are always free to go off-script, remember, whatever the sanctions provoked within the discipline of a class).

We then moved on to ask the performers to do any action they choose, and then check to see what the response was. Here, there is no script for the actions, but there are some conditions which determine the performer's response to that of the spectator.[2]

Next, we can use the exercise to work with what we recognize more conventionally as scripts: bits of prepared action and/or speech, where performers are assigned specific tasks, actions, words, responses, in specific places and times. This will resemble the point we reached in the previous exercise 'act when it's funny' and its variants. In this exercise, the performer(s) will do their script when onstage, but then exit when the audience response so dictates, then attempt to return, and so on.

We can do the On/Off exercise with all kinds of scripts, such as:

- simple actions and activities;
- simple linear tasks;
- multi-role actions or tasks.

For ways to approach different kinds of scripts, have a look back at the previous section.

5.4.1 On/Off with a funny plan

This same format can be used with 'funny plans', which are just scripts intended to make us laugh. See the previous section for some basic ideas on this. For full details on funny plans, see Part Three of this book.

5.4.2 On/Off with scripts in divergent modes

Once we have got used to these different kinds of plans, and using them in performance whilst responding in the moment to spectators' responses, we can try the same as earlier, with a pair of performers in opposite modes:

- Performer A does the plan when spectators laugh (and exits when they don't).
- Performer B does the plan when spectators don't laugh (and exits when they do).

This won't work with all scripts, as some are too complex or physically impossible to mess around with in this fashion. No matter, keep trying all the variants with different combinations, and you will discover ideas that work well for you, whilst discarding anything that is awkward or of no interest. Ideas are free and don't accumulate waste when discarded!

Once you get comfortable with all of this, you can play it more 'free-form'.

84 THE CLOWNING WORKBOOK

- In 3s: at least one person must decide to go on or off when audience laughter *changes* (it either starts or stops).
- Aim to respond **immediately** to the audience response.
- As soon as we laugh or stop laughing, cease doing whatever you're doing.
- Don't make decisions in the middle of audience laughter or silence (as old-school comedians used to say, the secret of comedy is not to interrupt the audience).

It's a conversation. In a normal conversation, you wouldn't keep talking when your interlocutor has started to respond, you would respond to their response. Unless you want to bore them and kill the dynamic relationship. If you are playing with a baby and making them laugh, you wouldn't insist on finishing your wonderfully creative idea, but instead would respond and take delight in the interaction.

Let us know that your responses are dependent on ours. It will feel as if you were 'thinking of us'.

In these exercises, the priority is this interaction, and not you or your creative content. The content, if there is any, is just a pretext for the conversation.

Figure 5 Step-Laugh: Kaisa Koskinen crossing the space.

6
STEP-LAUGH

The exercise Step-Laugh has been seminal in my own evolution as a clown teacher. It was a bridge between my experiences as a student (ending with Gaulier[1]) and my independent work as a teacher, which drew on some of the principles I had studied but became a completely different style. Later there came more specifically designed exercises using laughter response. In this section I will expand on how the basic Step-Laugh can be fruitfully applied and adapted across a wide range of performance training. The concern here will be on its adaptability, rather than on the basic exercise.[2]

The basic exercise goes like this:

6.1 Step-Laugh – crossing the stage

- One person crosses the stage, while the rest are their audience.

- The 'stage' is any space which a group of spectators can watch and understand as limited by its outer edges.[3] It can be marked out by screens, curtains, a door, or any starting and ending points you choose.

- The person crossing is dependent on the audience's response. When they laugh, the performer advances one step. When they don't laugh (for, say around six seconds), the performer moves back one step in their journey.

- Once the other side is reached, the exercise is over.

Teaching tips:

- The aim is to be accurate: to respond to the audience as and when they react.

88 THE CLOWNING WORKBOOK

- The aim is NOT to cross as quick as possible. The time taken is irrelevant.

- One might presume, actually, that a performer would desire to spend as much time as possible in the middle of the stage – isn't that why we do it?

- However, what may well happen is that the person will feel pressure to 'succeed' (i.e. get the laughs as quick as possible to get to the other side). The exercise is setting them up to assume this. And that is its value. We start with an assumption of how we might succeed, but then work on letting go of that desire, in order to revel in the pleasure of simply responding. Like a barometer.

- The exercise can be set up in two ways, if you wish:

  1 Request that the person does only the stated action, which is walking (and looking where they are going, where they have come from or at their audience).

  2 Suggest that the person tries any manner of things in order to test whether the audience responds with a laugh or a silence. In this case, you will need to be extra aware that you don't become attached to the results. Think of them as scientific probes: 'what happens if I do x? hmmm, interesting, silence . . .'.

- If you find that we laugh when you step backwards (it is common, probably due to the backward step being a staging in reality of your failure to provoke a laugh – in other words, it's a flop), then try and use what you do in this backward movement, and use it deliberately to see if we will laugh, thereby leading to a forward step.

If you're funny when you go back, then you should use that to go forwards. Can you convert what happens to you when you lose, fail, when you're not funny (but then funny because of that flop), to make us laugh? Can you go forwards using your backwards feeling? It will take a while to get this assimilated. When you go back, often we take pleasure in your feeling. So play those feelings.

STEP-LAUGH 89

In the beginning, your feeling might seem out of your control, perhaps negative and unwanted, when you step back because there is no laugh. But by paying continuous attention to what you are doing/feeling when stepping back (if we laugh on that step-back), by the end of the exercise you may find that your backward (funny) and forward (funny) steps are similar.

If you get good at doing this, you can even begin with this feeling, and start already 'in the flop':

- Can you start, from nothing, with that 'fail feeling' that we take pleasure in witnessing?
- Go straight to your manipulative, playful, feeling performance.

Pay attention also to when you feel 'I don't know why you're laughing'. This is also often a pleasure for us and makes us laugh. This is a good reason for just responding to the laughter and not asking 'why?'

Was it real, or not? Seems so. Oh, I'll play this, I'll take my confused feeling and pretend. At the point when we don't believe you anymore, we stop laughing. You don't have to worry about being fake, you can be fake as long as it's funny and when it stops being funny you just stop doing it. As an actor, you can play real, pretend real, declare it as fake. All these are valid.

The step-back as an apology

The backwards step is a kind of staging of an apology. It reads as a retreat, the beginning of an admission that you don't get to continue onstage, an actor's punishment. This emerges from the set-up of the exercise, where you look attached to going 'forwards' and not wanting to go 'backwards'. But it's silly, it doesn't matter.

Does it feel too much for you when people don't laugh at you? How to deal with it? As in other exercises, try saying 'sorry' (for not being funny). What happens now when you step back and say sorry?

Or perhaps you never get to hardly step on the stage? No worries! Some clowns are funny by not being onstage! In many classical entrées for a trio of clowns, one member of the trio isn't there for the first part of the number. Firstly, a duo spend time setting up the whole drama, and much later the third clown comes in, near the end to get the biggest laugh. Or then there is the clown who doesn't come on when presented. Or the climax to many circus numbers which is to be chased out.[4] So there's nothing traumatic about being offstage, at least for a clown. Try voicing it, from offstage: 'can I come on?'

6.2 Step-Laugh scripts

A key point to note here is that the task (crossing the stage) is already scripted (by the teacher). All kinds of other scripts can be substituted here, as in other exercises. Complex, theatrical scripts, abstract, physical-visual ones, whatever you choose. But the relationship with the audience is not scripted in the sense of being able to be written down as a text. The exercise Step-Laugh is a model for that in-the-moment relationship. It produces it, rather than prescribing it. It is a mechanism, a mode of relationship.[5]

This dynamic, where each step depends upon audience laughter, can easily be extended into more complex scripts than just crossing a stage. Now, one must divide up one's task into 'steps', each of which needs a laugh for the performer to be able to continue with their performance. In a rough way, then, this concept of 'steps' comes to be broadly analogous to Stanislavskian 'actions' (that which I do in order to achieve my task), or 'bits' ('beats' in the US). This converts the exercise into a multi-use technique for calibrating performance in a dialogue with the spectators' laughter response, lending itself to public performance as much as to learning the flop in workshops.

Practice and Theory
The exercise is eminently practical, and stems from hours and hours of exploration. Although it begins from that same question we've already referred to that Lecoq posed –'the clown makes us laugh, but how?' – yours own interpretation of what is going on in this exercise is quite different to the way in which Lecoq, and many since, theorized similar clown training exercises.

From my point of view, it stages two aspects of us at once. One part is that which wants to achieve something and, when we don't, we feel emotions that we experience as negative. The other part is that which realizes that it makes no difference in which direction we travel. Why would stage left be better than stage right, anyway? Being comfortable in this second attitude won't eliminate our feelings, but it will allow for a distance from them, leading to a lightness, pleasure, or whichever term you prefer to name how you want to perform. This is quite a different conclusion to Lecoq's, which led him to theorize the 'personal clown'.

And although the exercise appears at first sight to be mechanical – in fact, it is in the sense that it lays bare the mechanics of a relationship between a clown and a spectator – its greatest fruits may lie in providing a frame for exploring our feelings while clowning. I will deal more directly with 'feelings' in the second part of the book, but it's inevitable that they arise.

CASE STUDY 6.1

Weekly clown course, London Clown School, June 2019

The weekly clown course ran almost uninterruptedly from 2015 onwards, as a rolling course. Some participants attended for lengthy periods of time, others dropped in when they were able to, either between performing or on their travels. London is by its nature a fluid place, where most people are from elsewhere in Britain or the world. Most probably this bore heavily on the way these classes developed, in a spirit of ongoing exploration. After some years, the format switched to finite one-term courses, but even then a large proportion of the exercises each term were new developments. In this sense, it has acted as a kind of laboratory for progressing clown training, the results of which then get drawn on in other workshops around the world.[6]

Here are some reflections which throw light on some of the variations and applications of the Step-Laugh exercise:

Solo Step-Laugh

Wait for that moment when you are about to feel shit, because it is when there is no laughter and everyone recognizes it, as it may be this moment when you look stupid and we laugh. Look out for these moments, that is the aim of this exercise.

6-Step Script with Chair

In this version, the 'script', instead of being 'cross the stage' is defined in 6 steps: enter; move to centre stage next to the chair placed there; sit on the chair; stand up from the chair; move to near the exit opposite to where you entered from; exit.

2-Person Step-Laugh

- This version has two people doing the exercise together, each moving when they feel that the audience has laughed at them. Curiously, students may often ask, or assume, that the two participants should begin at opposite sides of the stage. There is nothing in the instructions which might lead them to this, so one can only guess that their assumptions come from outside of the training, almost certainly from an inculcated sense of symmetry or 'fairness'. It can't be said too often, fairness is not a productive approach in clowning!

- There's something about two people being on the same path, in the same task, that demands that one tell the other what to do. It's normal. What's not normal is agreeing on everything and saying yes to everything.[7]

- Voice your feeling when it starts to well up.[8]

Own scripts

In this version, two participants have had some time to write their own script prior to doing the exercise in front of others. The script should consist of clearly composed 'steps', that can be executed in reality.

- In a sequence based on moving to points on the stage, it is obvious that each point moved to must be possible, in that it will be somewhere you move to from the point you are already at. It is impossible to have gaps in this sequence. You cannot move from where you are not.

- Likewise, when you come to make more abstract scripts, move to the next step from where you are. In a narrative, that is easy. But it also applies to something abstract.

Counting as a technique

- It's not uncommon to get confused in this simple exercise. Confused by what? Your own thoughts, feelings, doubts, they sometimes become too much to cope with. In order to clear your head, try counting – in your head, not out loud or on fingers as a means to make us laugh, although this is also legitimate.

- When waiting for the audience response, count six seconds. Or a different number. Each individual might work better with a different number of seconds. Try five, two, nine, whatever.

What the action of counting does is several things:

- Takes your mind off you feeling shit because no one is laughing.
- Blocks you from doing actions that only divert you, which come from shit feelings and trying to cover and conceal them.
- Stops you trying continually to make us laugh.
- Focuses you on our response rather than on your 'self'.

Counting 'cleanses' your approach, blocking avoidance behaviour and re-focusing on the task, which is to carry out the simple action of a step whilst paying attention to spectators' responses. This detaches you from the obligation of doing the action, whilst still doing the action, which remains obligatory. This obligation, 'to act', is what puts you in that difficult, shit position. The script, in obliging you to do it, puts you 'onstage' and necessarily leads to you feeling something under the gaze of the audience. These feelings, of being judged funny or not, are inescapable perhaps, but you don't have to remain attached to them. All this avoids acting just by habit or on impulse (which may be the same thing). It avoids the trap of improvisation, which is to frequently just repeat what we've done many times before.

Speaking your feelings

Another way to detach yourself from the 'shit feelings' is simply to speak them. They then become performed, played and detached from you.

Looking at the audience

If you've experienced even just a small amount of clown training over the past several decades, you have almost certainly come across the command to 'look at the audience'. The act of sharing eye contact with spectators has become axiomatic to clowning. I myself have mostly been enthusiastic and can recall many times thinking I had to constantly prompt students to do so whilst in the middle of exercises.

In Step-Laugh, a good starting guide can be to split your gaze 50/50 between the audience, and what's happening onstage (one foot in the reality of the auditorium, one foot in the fiction of the play, as it were). But there comes a time when this 'rule' falls by the wayside. Anyway, it is only a guide, a way to get used to living equally in those two worlds. But it will not always apply in practice. It will depend on many factors, the venue, the individual performer's style or personality.

In Step-Laugh it can be useful or necessary to introduce some more specific instructions to help individual students.

Further variations

When the attention to the audience's response becomes well-tuned, any number of variations can be played out, in any kind of spatial configuration:

- Cross a circle.
- Move on hearing laughter, in the dark.

Some variations will bring to the fore the ways in which audience and clown tie themselves together:

- Move towards the laughter (this suggests that the 'script' was to leave or cross the stage, but something more interesting has emerged, the relationship with spectators).
- Make your objective 'to leave the stage' (by suppressing the audience's laughter).

CASE STUDY 6.2

Five-day workshop, Brussels, November 2019

Jon (**to JG** <u>while doing the exercise</u>)   Don't look at the audience while waiting for our laugh 'decision'. But then, when there is no laugh, you look at the audience exactly as you start your backwards step. And then you continue to look at us during that step, until you have come to rest again, and then your next six-second cycle begins.

After the exercise:

JG   Why?

Jon   Previously, you were looking at us a lot while waiting for our judgement, and that looking transmitted the fear, the anxiety, the desire and attachment to being liked and given permission to advance. This is not pleasurable for anyone. By being prohibited from looking at us, you are forced to 'be alone', as it were, during these moments. And it seems like you let go of your anxiety. But then, when it is time for you to act, you look at us and share your feeling of 'yes, you're right, I have failed and must go back', which is pleasurable for us, endearing and funny. And so you advance a step again. There is a lesson for all here: share your failure, not your anxiety.

CASE STUDY 6.3

Weekend workshop, Brighton November 2019

Acting feelings

Sometimes, when undergoing these kinds of exercises, we assume we know what kind of feelings should be accompanying the key moments when you enter, progress, go back, leave – happiness, disappointment, embarrassment, etc. and then we try and act those emotions at the points we deem correct. This might happen especially when the performer isn't actually feeling much at all, and then tries to slot in an acted emotion to take the place of the supposedly absent one. Although it probably won't be the case that they are not feeling anything at this moment. Instead, they may be feeling confused things, suppressed feelings. It doesn't matter too much what. The point is to move away and create some distance. If this substitution emotion is happening, know that really it's better just to leave a gap there.

There is a related phenomenon which, oddly, appears to be the opposite of the preceding one:

JH   I tried at the start to be neutral, spontaneous, whatever arises. But nothing happens. It's like I can't be blamed if it's not funny.

Jon   And then I demanded you try and be funny, to try harder.

JH   Yes, and then I felt I can be blamed for it not working.

In this case, the supposed 'neutral' is simply a cover for holding back from feeling.

'Try harder': it's not a phrase that crops up often in clown training these days. More often than not, the binary opposite 'don't try' will be uttered (another one of those assumptions we tend not to question).[9] But if, like the above student, we try to 'stay neutral', we don't commit to the purpose of the clown enough to be able to have a flop. Clearly, 'trying harder' isn't enough in itself, you must also recognize when your attempt is failing, otherwise we just have the painful experience of watching someone insisting they are funny when they are not.

Additionally, in line with my own personal preference for contrariness, I like to use the word 'try' as it supposedly belongs to that kind of pedagogy that we are supposed to reject nowadays, based on merit, talent, or effort (at least in the world of contemporary clowning). And it fits with how I like to play with notions such as judgement, punishment, good, bad, etc. Trying to 'neutralize' by turning away from these things, in the belief that emancipation from power structures can be wished away, only leads to dullness at best. And it's much more fun to play with them!

CASE STUDY 6.4

Clowning and puppetry workshop, April 2019, London

This workshop was an experiment to see how much the two genres of puppetry and clowning could crossover or have in common. It was jointly run by myself and Jum Faruq, who is a puppeteer and also well versed in clowning, who trained and performed with me among others.

We split the workshop into alternating sections, with a puppetry warm-up, a clown warm-up, a foundation exercise in each and then some attempts to bring both together. The Step-Laugh exercise proved very effective when working with bunraku puppets. Bunraku puppets have three people operating them, one controlling the neck/head and one hand/arm, one holds the other arm and the waist, and the other taking the feet. In the workshop the puppets are made of brown paper rolled up and formed into a kind of 'stick figure' that is flexible.

- As with the basic Step-Laugh exercise, there was a pre-scripted route, which on this occasion was from offstage (behind a column) to a 'centre stage' a place in the middle of the space in front of a step, which naturally drew our attention as the focal point in the space.
- It was the paper bunraku puppet who would trace these steps, with its three puppeteers responding to spectators' laughter or absence of laughter to move forwards or backwards.

Some unique obstacles presented themselves, but which, on close inspection, did resemble some of the issues encountered by human participants in this exercise. When the puppet does (is made to do) off-script stuff, it's hard for us to read it. This could be:

- things to make us laugh;
- or 'acting' that tries to commentate on the situation;
- or, as above, attempting to substitute the presumed appropriate emotion expression.

On a simple level, this may well be due to the intentions of a 3-person puppet being confused, at least in this situation where three people, unfamiliar to each other, are called upon to try an exercise they have never done before.

But what about the version of the exercise described earlier, where the attempt to be funny is encouraged? Isn't that possible for a puppet? Perhaps yes with practised puppeteers, but again the problem is the lack of clarity of intention ('to be funny'). How do we know when a puppet is 'trying to be funny'?

Likewise, with a person, there are all sorts of micro-reactions that you have, whilst attempting the exercise. These reactions are connected to your feelings, your real feelings about being in this real situation in front of real people (they are 'stage emotions'). But puppets cannot have these feelings, in this semi- or uncontrolled manner. With a person, those off-script bits are unfiltered, spontaneous even. But the puppet doesn't have those bits of behaviour which indicate 'I am feeling stupid'. The puppet can do stupid things, but not 'behave stupidly'.

On the other hand, the intention to go to a point in the space is clear. Both for a human and for a puppet. In conclusion, as humans we might take as our model a puppet!

Unique to the puppets seemed to be how spectators were fascinated by the puppet having plenty of tension so that the disagreement between puppeteers and bits of body can be clearly read. This then mirrors a person's split feelings of wanting to go to point X but not knowing if they can, of trying but failing.

CASE STUDY 6.5

DH Ensemble, April 2019, London

The DH Ensemble is a theatre company comprised of Deaf and Hearing actors. Using Step-Laugh and other clown exercises in coaching this ensemble revealed some exciting discoveries about clowning.

Not all deaf actors will respond similarly, obviously, but in general when asked to respond to laughter, certain things will happen which at least seem to be less frequent than with most hearing actors. Hearing actors usually assume that laughter is only ever perceived through hearing. Deaf actors, though, will potentially have more ways to perceive it.

With the mixed group of actors, then, the manner in which each individual sought to ascertain if and when spectators were laughing had a large impact on what those actors were 'doing'. The action, or script, was profoundly influenced by the act of attending to audience laughter. And this is one of the things which is exciting about clowning. One might almost say that clowns' actions are driven fundamentally by their attention to the spectator. Or, even, *created* by that attention.

When interpreters were also involved in the communications between deaf and hearing actors and the spectators, then the dynamics of communication impacted even more on the action.

The clowning came to be 'about' those relationships. Unavoidably, that's where we were led.

CASE STUDY 6.6

MA Shakespeare Studies, Shakespeare's Globe, London, December 2009

When the place of performance has very particular characteristics, this exercise can help immensely in rooting out points of focus and establishing a basis for performer/audience interaction and communication.

The main purpose of this workshop was to teach basic clowning to the students on the MA in Shakespeare Studies. I was also interested to find out how clown works in the Globe, and how clown teaching works in this space. I wouldn't address the very particular question of actual clown roles in Shakespeare, but instead explore what clown training can offer to the actor. The principal question is, what embodied knowledge and techniques can the clown-actor advantageously bring to the particular conditions of the Globe stage?

Clowning starts with some advantages in this space, as one of the keys to clowning is the immediate and here-and-now contact with the audience and the space. The clown is a master of direct address. Without this complicity, the clown is nothing, as their performance must take off without reliance on character or plot (though these may co-exist with the clown). This helps not just the roles denominated as 'clowns', but any performer in the particular space.

Some conclusions from our explorations using Step-Laugh at the Globe were:

- The Globe is at once a complex space and one constructed with a simple purpose.
- There are so many places, nooks, crannies, sightlines, up, down around nearly 360 degrees.
- But all with the intention of entering into a clear, daylight interactive dynamic conversation between players and spectators.[10]
- The Globe has much in common with the circus, and also with the street.
- Responding to audience responses in the moment is relatively simple.

When the Globe opened, many actors and directors were afraid they weren't prepared for such an interactive, daylight experience with their audiences. But the Globe's director, Mark Rylance, intuitively understood how an audience dialogues with the actors in the act of story-telling.[11]

This dialogue between performers and spectators has been ironed out in much of Western theatre practice, but it survives in many popular forms of culture, from story-telling to call-and-answer prayers. For clowning specialists, what Preiss calls 'Interlocution' is both historically and practically fundamental.[12]

7
THAT WAS/N'T FUNNY

One evening, a few classes into a weekly course at London Clown School with a very lively and enthusiastic group of students, it occurred to me that the whole clown learning process might be a lot simpler than it is often claimed to be. Although there's a lot to be said for searching for the subtleties of clowning which, when 'found', elicit our reactions of 'ah yes, that's it!', this reliance on what feels mysterious or unreachable can be a frustrating obstacle in the learning process, for both students and teachers. There is a more brutally direct, and more objective route, which comes when we ask the question 'was that funny, or not?' The following exercise emerged from such ponderings.

7.1 Catching the ball in a circle

- All stand in a circle and throw and catch a small ball.

- The receiver says, after catching it (or missing it, as is the case), 'that was funny' or 'that wasn't funny'. The choice of which phrase to say is dictated by whether there was laughter in the room or not.

- The receiver then throws the ball to someone else.

- If there is initially no laughter after a receiver has got the ball, and they have already said 'that wasn't funny', but then there is laughter after the receiver has spoken, but before they throw the ball again, then that receiver should say 'that was funny'.

That sounds simple, but as we human beings love to make things more complicated, here are some things to look out for and avoid.

Common issues:

- The receiver doesn't speak.
- Someone other than the receiver says something. Avoid this and be concerned with what happens when you speak after your catch. It's all about the reaction to the completed action, the catcher is the person upon whom the 'judgement' falls.
- Saying something else.
- Saying something which didn't happen (lying), trying to be ironic.

Just observe and record accurately.

The act of speaking the judgement exteriorizes the feelings and declaration of what we all witness and know to be true. There is nowhere to hide, and no shame.

7.2 Catching the ball for an audience

- Three players play the game as before, but facing everyone else, who are their audience.
- Split your attention roughly equally between co-players and audience.

7.3 Any action in a circle

- All stand in a circle again.
- Any one person can do any small action, stepping a little into the circle as they do so, then retiring back to their place.
- The person who has done the action says 'that was funny' or 'that wasn't funny', after they have completed their action.
- If more than one person steps up, just carry on as a duo or trio, but aim for solos as far as possible.

7.4 Any action for an audience

- Three players play this latest version, but facing everyone else, who are their audience.

Teaching notes

- The aim here should be on building the connection between
    1 what you just did, and
    2 how others reacted. and then externalizing it by speaking.
- It's irrelevant whether people laugh or not, or whether you think you are funny, or not funny. That is all bypassed by concentrating on the response and then responding to that.
- The process is one of conditioning, not of 'discovery'.

7.5 This is going to be funny

Once this starts to become automatic (note: we already have automatic, habitual responses, and this is simply replacing those with something useful for clowning), then it's likely you are having fun, or finding things funny, instead of having a bad time struggling to be liked by your peers. At least that's the hope!

It may happen that you start to feel some pleasurable anticipation of whether what you are about to do will elicit a laughing or a non-laughing response. This feeling may express itself as your own laughter, just before or as you begin your action. If this happens, now you can say

- 'This is going to be funny'.
- ONLY say this if you genuinely have some such feeling or laughter.
- DON'T say this in some hope that it might be funny, or as an ironic comment.
- After your action, speak as previously, recognizing what others actually responded with. It doesn't matter whether your 'this is going to be funny' turns out to be the case or not.
- NEVER say 'this *isn't* going to be funny'.

Objective/Subjective

The first stages of this exercise rely on us speaking the 'objective truth': what we observe others to be doing (laughing or not laughing). Although we can obviously make a mistake in our observations (not realize, hear something that didn't happen), most people in the room will be in agreement. In this way we stay faithful to only stating that which is objectively true.

But isn't the latest version, predicting what might happen, subjective? Not really, in that your spoken observation is of your own feeling, which, unless you are lying, is most certainly objectively true. You are simply saying the truth about how you feel, even though that feeling is about something yet to happen.

7.6 Extended variations

- When your action elicits a laughter response and after you have said 'that was funny', repeat your action and speak again accordingly with either 'that was funny again' or 'that's still funny', or, if no laughter ensues this time, 'that's not funny anymore'.
- This is a form of 'exhausting the laughter'.

Trying to be funny

As with the previous exercise, we can play this one at different levels of 'trying'. Your actions can be simple, even abstract, with no intention to provoke laughter. Or they can be with maximum intention to do so. In both cases, and everything in between, the mechanism is identical: action – response – response.

It will be up to the individual, their style, their preferences, their overall intentions, just where on that scale they will finally place themselves.

The taboo around 'trying' probably isn't limited to being funny or comedy in general. Actor trainers have frequently pontificated on the dangers of trying to deliberately evoke or express any kind of emotion. Much contemporary actor training, including clowning, generally goes along with this axiom unthinkingly, in a lineage which certainly includes Stanislavski[1], but also those whose work has leaned heavily on games and 'play', such as Jacques Copeau or Howard Barker.[2] The implication

THAT WAS/N'T FUNNY

in this play-based philosophy is usually that play is a means to avoid 'cabotinage', or 'ham acting'.[3] The danger is where these assumptions become invisible, unthinking rules.[4]

If this 'not trying but playing' slips into an assumption that clowning is 'just supposed to happen', then it neutralizes the expectations of the genre.[5] Ironically, given that Lecoq's sole assumption originally was that clowns are supposed to make us laugh. Clowning can happen anytime, but without the expectations of clowning it is a whole different enterprise. And often much more difficult to achieve. Unless our expectations are to laugh at a ridiculous human (clown) on a stage, then it is unlikely that this will happen. Genre expectations are the starting point for performance forms of all types. As we shall see, the attempt to be funny will actually increase the clown's chances of failing to be funny, thence being funny as a result. The famous 'Flop'.

CASE STUDY 7.1

Weekend workshop, Brussels, November 2019

Notes on the lure and dangers of symmetry

The following events could have occurred during many exercises, especially those which ask for a few volunteers to take the stage in front of a seated audience. In this case, it was while doing the exercise which concerns us in this section, 'That was/n't funny'.

Three volunteers go up to do the next exercise, as requested.

They back up, to form a straight line facing us.

I repeat my observation that they stepped back already (from the previous work with the exercise Ball Tag). I ask:

Why?

We haven't started yet.

But why did you do that?

To be ready.

Why in a line?

Why not?

But why? There must be a reason you chose this formation.

It's neutral. We don't want to prejudge the outcome, but be here and then see what happens.

Why would you want that?

To see what emerges naturally.

Why would you want that outcome?

This neatly illustrates the ingrained assumption that the best clowning (and performance in general) is supposed to 'just happen', as long as we don't interfere or 'prejudge'. Ironically, though, the forming of a straight line at the start of the exercise does precisely this: it prejudges and pre-sets the potential outcome and erases other potential events.

The conversation continued:

Is that a potentially clown choice or outcome? I mean, is it likely to be funny, stupid, or ridiculous?

No, but we haven't started.

When we started the workshop, I said, let's start clowning immediately. Why not now?

. . .

I'm just asking you to reflect and question yourselves: are my choices clown choices? And if not, then why not? And what clown choices could I make? Because, although you give the excuse of not having started, it shows that your primary choices are not clown ones. When you are performing, what's to stop you making more of these non-clown choices, especially if you feel under pressure? I bet you will make these non-clown choices later on, once you HAVE started. I guarantee it. For sure!

This conversation might have gone on for more than five minutes, it feels like ten minutes.

People are getting angry in the workshop.

OK, let's carry on with the exercise.

The three students are focused on avoiding the straight line, after this ten-minute debate. Phew, I think, it WAS worth it! Then suddenly, they form a straight line. The audience groans instantly! The performers realize, and correct themselves. The conditioning is beginning to work!

Next three volunteers: they take up positions on the stage to begin. They ostentatiously avoid the straight line. They are standing in a triangle, one of them centre stage downstage, the other two at the sides upstage.

OK, that's also very symmetrical. Is it a clown choice?

Hmmm. . . .

OK, no triangles allowed!

They try to avoid the symmetrical shape of a triangle, but it's not so easy. But fairly quickly, they form up with two close to each other and the third one at a distance. Yes. It's a classic duo and outsider relationship. The exercise then develops quickly, as long as they maintain their spatial relationship. The 'loner' wants to take charge, proposing things. When it's funny, the duo take it up and repeat it, and then it's not funny. Conversely, when the soloist flops, and the duo repeat their flop, it's funny! So we have a clear set of relationships that drives our pleasure in watching this unfold.

CASE STUDY 7.2

Calgary Clown Festival, Canada, September 2019

This week-long workshop took place in a large, well-equipped theatre, with sizeable backstage areas and auditorium. The temptation to 'be in the right place' in this imposing venue seemed to lie heavily on us at times. The 'right place' being somewhere vaguely 'centre stage' so that presumably everyone can see and hear you.

These conventional restrictions may serve the actor in search of balance, but clowns surely seek more imbalance?

If your partner is 'working', if what they are doing is amusing us and engaging our attention, feel free to wander around, according to how you feel. Don't feel obliged to stand there.

Wander the space, unconstrained by usual actor concerns to get things right in this 'magical' space: you don't need to worry about lighting cues, blocking, text, audience, rhythm. The space is just a building, it's not magical for clowns. Destroy the magic!

Such discussions and experimentation led to some daring choices that enhanced the clowning, with performers disappearing backstage or making lots of noise, or emerging with surprising objects. The possibilities were endless.

More on speaking and silent clowns

As noted in the previous section, sometimes there is a belief that speaking isn't appropriate in clowning. It's probably once again the association of the intellect with the word, the so-called 'tyranny of the text'. The immediate post-war period found these ideas useful in pushing back against what was viewed as an overly brainy, disembodied performance culture. The whole Lecoquian enterprise presumes that the body in movement precedes speech and thought. But times change.

Our lopsidedly literate culture assumes words to be associated with thought. Oral forms of performance know that the act of speaking is indeed an action, and one with real consequences. Here, the consequences are a public recognition of what we all perceive to be true. When we speak, when we sound, and even more so when we verbalize those sounds into a comprehensible phrase, we take the biggest risk of all. The risk of appearing foolish. When we commit our thoughts, feelings and impulses to words, there feels like there is no going back, no retraction. Speech is held to be that upon which we may be judged. As truth-tellers or liars. Of course, our actions may also be judged. But there is a special place for the spoken word. Oral cultures hold that that which is spoken is law. Whereas that which is only written down cannot ever have the same authority.[6] The exercise in this section plainly relies 100% on this act of speech.

Besides, the history of clowns shows us a rich variety of clowns who speak, don't speak and much in between, depending on the material conditions of their performing spaces (large three-ring arenas imposed silence, amplified sound allowed for speaking, radio necessitated it) and many other factors.[7]

Figure 6 Three on a Bench: Athena Amoret, Giedre Degutyte, Kaisa Koskinen.

8
MAKE OTHERS INTO CLOWNS

This is a little diversion which can emerge from any of the previous exercises which begins throwing and catching the ball in a circle. It developed fully during regular weekly classes at London Clown School and London Metropolitan University in 2019–20.

8.1 Throw ball with intention

- Throw/catch the ball in a circle.
- Ask yourself: 'what response am I desiring to have from the receiver, after the ball has left my hand and I **no longer have any control over it**?'

This question may puzzle some, as you may be concerned with what YOU are doing, rather than on someone else and their reaction. This exercise asks you to focus on the other, not on yourself.

Note: most mainstream clown training of the past 50 years has asked you to focus on yourself, so this may take some time to get used to. On the other hand, it is an easy and natural instinct to follow once you realize where to find it.

You can't actually control or determine the receiver's response, as no one can ever control another. But you can have an intention, and maybe have some success in provoking your desired response.

Is your intention to:

- Elicit a smile?
- Make them annoyed?
- Make them look stupid?

Play again, and:

- If the catcher does respond how you (the thrower) intended, raise your hand.
- Next, the catcher must try to subvert the expectations and intentions of the thrower.
- It's now a kind of clown competition, where each tries to make the other look stupid.

Now, play again but

- With the sole intention of eliciting laughter in the room when the receiver receives the ball (NOT when you throw it).
- This exercise will remain difficult for you if you continue to focus on your own creativity or trying to make yourself laughable. You have to redirect the laughter onto another.

In this exercise, clowning is goal-oriented: you have an intention, that may or may not be achieved. When you throw the ball in such a way that you make the receiver our object of laughter, your thoughts are directed to this task. Not to being funny, or throwing it funnily, but to provoking or eliciting a reaction, from us spectating.

To make it even richer:

- Don't catch the ball when it's funny (when there is laughter).

8.2 Don't catch it when it's funny

- Throw/catch.
- You're out if you're holding the ball when there is laughter.

MAKE OTHERS INTO CLOWNS 113

- In threes, for an audience (you can have several lives in order to make it last a little bit longer).
- Now re-introduce the strong intention to provoke the catcher, play as above, in threes facing an audience.
- Add the rule: you cannot avoid catching the ball, even when there is laughter.
- Dispense with the ball: use any means you wish to make your friends look stupid, direct our laughter at them.

This leaves the players with a set of options, as follows. If you have the ball, you can:

- Not throw it and risk the others make you funny so you lose lives.
- Try and pass it to someone else but they will probably refuse, leaving you at risk.

If you don't have the ball, you can:

- Try and avoid being passed the ball and keep the owner at risk.
- Catch the ball.

Observations: if we then stop and ask ourselves about what we just saw, what do these three people look like? What do we, the audience, think about them?

- X looks more stupid than Y.
- Even though Z looks more intelligent, Z keeps losing.

Conclusions
Clowning doesn't have to be personal. You can make your friend the object of laughter whilst maintaining both your statuses as clowns. This can verge on the extreme, when someone appears to have a talent for making others look stupid. How do you draw the audience's attention to your victim?

Or it can be via a set-up, where the mise-en-scène produces the clowns. Who might not even be persons.

CASE STUDY 8.1

London Metropolitan University, BA Theatre and Performance, 2019

In this case, the group advanced rapidly having a good level of interplay and trust, allowing for ever more complex variations. Groups of three were able to perform the exercise for the audience, not with the ball-throwing as their script, nor with improvised actions, but with prepared scenes/scripts. The aim was to play the script while trying to make each other the object of laughter.

Script plans which were easy for us to follow were better, as we could focus on the attention drawing, not on the plot.

If the plan has a built-in bias towards picking on each other, then be aware that this is not the only structure for the exercise. It doesn't have to match the plan's format.

In order to play the game, break out of the fictional world of your plan. For example, one group devised a scene involving playing a parent and child and teacher. Initially this played out as a seated dialogue, but they didn't have to stay on chairs talking, they could do anything to draw laughs to each other: balance on a chair, be outrageous in an anachronistic way.

CASE STUDY 8.2

London Clown School weekly class, 2019

One group had devised a plan which was a slow motion race. This proved difficult for them to execute in this exercise, because it was hard to break away from the agreement to do slow motion (fiction), and thence to find options to make each other look ridiculous. I think it's because the mime imposes an extra level of 'agreement' which is unreal, thus blocking our 'natural' instincts to disrupt, be mean, play tricks. They tried again with real running and it was much easier.

MAKE OTHERS INTO CLOWNS

More conclusions

- Remember, first focus on the laughs. Once you can do that, then you can reflect on how you feel, on what you are thinking. If you focus on yourself first, we just get a boring ego on stage. And we don't want that.

- Be accurate. Once you start doing something, don't think 'oh I hope I can continue', instead think, 'when are they going to tell me to stop by ceasing laughing?'

- By directing your thinking outwards, projecting it onto our response to someone else, you may think less about yourself. This is good.

9
LAUGHTER AS A PARDON

In my own teaching, the concept and practice of the pardon arose very early on in the exercises using a rolled-up newspaper to 'punish' someone when, for example, they drop the ball in a ball game, or lose a game of tag. This is, of course, classic Gaulier. If we add the proviso of 'if you lose or fail but we laugh, then you won't get punished', the function of laughter as pardon becomes immediately obvious.[1]

On one level, this is just one instance of conditioning a response to laughter: they laugh, I feel pardoned. We could pair up lots of stage choices, some of which we have already looked at, with the occurrence of laughter, for example, when there is laughter, . . .

- Throw the ball
- Don't throw the ball
- Cross the circle
- Take a step
- Don't take a step
- Sit down
- Stand up
- Move
- Be still
- Go behind the screen
- Come out from behind the screen
- Say 'thank you'

- Say 'shut up'
- Smile
- Frown.

These are perhaps familiar, either from our knowledge of clowns or comedians on stages, or from our interpersonal engagements. But we could try others, which may not occur in the course of our lives otherwise, like:

- Speak
- Sing
- Dance
- Eat chocolate
- Sleep
- Die
- Have sex.

And so on. 'Make up your own.'

But, for now, let's explore a little more the way 'pardon' might help us in the practice of clowning.

Predication on laughter

In general in this book, I am curious about what particular outcomes occur when we pay attention to laughter. In this section, how does this attention bear upon exercises, and in particular some children's games used as exercises, when the conditioned response to the laughter is a pardon, immunity or permission to come back?

9.1 Ball Tag

This is an exercise I have worked with and written about for some time.[2] Here I want to look at how it can be used as further training for conditioning in responding to an audience.

Firstly, a short summary on the basic game and how it functions:

LAUGHTER AS A PARDON 119

- There is one ball, and if it hits you on the knees or below, you are out of the game. Last person left wins.
- This is all the instructions or rules you need to play this game. Everything else is up for grabs.
- What mostly happens is someone will get the ball and throw it at someone to try and get them out. Then someone else (or the same person) gets the ball and tries to get someone else out. And so on.
- Generally, people run away, at first. But then realize there are 'clever' strategies for winning, like hiding or restraining others.

Variations and extra rules can include:

- A trio plays for an audience, splitting their eye contact and attention 50/50 between game and audience.
- The players have several lives, only being out completely when they have lost all of them.
- No reverse movement allowed (i.e. you always have to move forwards).
- Use an 'imaginary ball instead of a real ball. (Who decides when the ball touches you?)
- Other parts of the body as target: chest, bottom, back.

9.1.1 Ball Tag with laughter conditioning

There are two simple ways to do this:

1 You can only throw the ball when there is laughter.
2 You cannot be out when there is laughter – including laughter that comes as a result of ball contact.

More simply put: no life can be lost while there is laughter.

Both axioms lead to the same outcomes and consequential behaviour, which commonly include:

THE CLOWNING WORKBOOK

- If I have the ball and want to get someone out, I have to stop the audience laughing in order to be able to throw the ball.
- If I don't have the ball and am at risk of being out, I have to provoke laughter in order to be safe.
- If I have just been hit by the ball, I have to instantly provoke laughter in order to be saved.

Some surprising strategies (in order to be safe when under threat, by eliciting laughter), emerge from all of this:

- Move forwards towards the audience.
- Look at the audience.

Both of these are kinds of opposites of some habitual responses to this 'danger' (mock danger in play). In 'normal' threat situations, we are more prone to:

- Move backwards.
- Not look up.

On the other hand, the new strategies do actually chime with behaviour which is familiar to us. This is easier to grasp by imagining a young child upset or afraid, looking to an adult carer for safety – they look at the adult and move towards them.

Whilst it's advisable not to take these parallels too far, the clown-as-scared-child is not a bad one to explore. If you find yourself desperate and anxious onstage, try appealing to the audience for help and comfort, rather than running away from them. They might love you for it!

Games are not theatre, nor clowning

A final tip for this game played for clowning purposes is that you are always free NOT to try and win, if that makes you more ridiculous and amusing (in the audience's eyes). If you hate competitive games, or in the moment just feel like being out, then 'be out!' If you pay attention to the audience response, you will know what to do next. You may find that we wanted you to lose, anyway. As long as you don't do anything to spoil our enjoyment, we will go along with it.

LAUGHTER AS A PARDON 121

This fact (and it's clearly observable that many times as a spectator we will love someone for not caring about the rules or objectives) demonstrates neatly how and why rule-bound games do not operate in the same way as clowning. Nor indeed as theatre.

9.2 Musical Chairs

This game is probably familiar to most in its basic form, though there may be extra rules or variations in different places where it's played by children:

- Sit on a chair when the music stops, anyone without a chair is out, remove chairs each round, last one left wins.

It's also fairly widespread in clown training, where its Gaulier-inspired versions give rise to more difficulty and confusion, either due to the controller's actions:

- The person in control of the music varies the way it stops – slow fade out, false stop and re-start, etc.
- The person in control of removing chairs each round removes several chairs at once (not just one) or none at all.

Or because of additional requirements when the music stops, before sitting down:

- Give someone a kiss.
- Kick someone's arse.
- Give one person a kiss and another person a kick.

Why use children's games?
As a fairly standard, fun activity, it gets you in a playful and naughty mood, enjoying losing, but that's it, it's just a preparation for something more. It doesn't actually get you to that 'more'.

Sometimes it's worth just doing something 'easy', though. Not all training has to be 'getting somewhere'. Children's games modified (as the above versions of Musical Chairs) fit that bill in this format, but we can also take that somewhere further. A simple thing to do is to add in the laughter as a pardon.

Now we have:

9.2.1 Musical Chairs with laughter conditioning

- Play Musical Chairs (with or without any of the modifications described above) but no-one can be out if there is laughter.
- You can state that the laughter will act as a saviour if it happens before the person who is out has left the playing space or sat down in the audience area.

As with Ball Tag, this quickly opens up specifically clownish strategies and behaviour, like:

- If you have no chair, you quickly do something to make your friends laugh – and maybe succeed, or not.
- You simply find that your unconscious reaction to losing makes you laughable.
- You 'milk' the loss as you leave the playing space.

And, as before, as in clowning there is no need to want to win a game:

- You do something to elicit laughter in order to save someone else who has lost.
- You deliberately lose and try to suppress everyone's laughter.

9.3 Grandmother's Footsteps with laughter conditioning

One of the first successful fusions of laughter conditioning with these kinds of games came in a workshop in Johannesburg in March 2018. A simpler way to get to Step-Laugh presented itself, by modifying Grandmother's Footsteps.

CASE STUDY 9.1

AFDA, Johannesburg, one-week workshop, March 2018

This group often felt like two groups in one, and as such had its own idiosyncratic way of functioning. Some of the dynamics one finds in more homogeneous groups weren't so present, while other bonds between participants came to the fore, based on age, experience, background, culture. This was clear from day one. Rather than seeing these differences as obstacles – let's remember, clowning is often about difference and misunderstanding rather than agreement and cohesion – the challenge was to find a path towards learning for everyone, that played to everyone's strengths.

Curiously, even the playing of the game of Grandmother's Footsteps seemed to present questions. Did the game demand a group 'agreement' to compete? What if there isn't that sense of group? Does it become difficult to play the competition? It seemed so to me.

The obvious conclusion to me at that moment, as a teacher, was that this aspect of the game wasn't going to function to teach anyone. The exercise as it stood didn't do its job. The next obvious observation was then: what if we remove the stipulation to compete? So that's what we did. Some students still played it to win, it was their preferred way to play. But others could then choose to lose, or disrupt the game, or just not play at all! It seemed to me that these options allowed for a lot more freedom, fun and transgression – all good objectives on a clown workshop.

Jon   The thing is, you don't have to win. You can really let go of competitive games. It's weird, I set you up with these games to win, then I pull the rug out from under you. Why is that?

It's a model for us as humans/clowns. The part that engages, is attached to tasks, success, achievement, desiring. First, we activate it, so it comes to the fore. Then we rebalance it with detachment, with a growing realization that I don't have to be wedded to all this. So a clown foregrounds all that attachment, only to then reveal that it's all a joke! Playing the game is a joke!

Interestingly, once we had embarked on this corrupted version of the game, new options began to present themselves more clearly. It occurred to me that now there was space (having voided it of competition) for other stipulations to come in. Such as:

- Only move forwards towards Grandmother when there is laughter.

Or:

- If Grandmother turns round and spots someone moving but we are laughing, those people can't be sent back, they can keep moving in full view of Grandmother.

This gave us some new strategies that brought out daring transgressive behaviour, like:

- Gamble on the laughter, take a step and if you get the laugh after, then OK and stay there. Otherwise, all the way back to the beginning.

Having played the game in these ways, it was very easy to then move onto the exercise Step-Laugh. It's the same principle, but without the competitive framework.

CASE STUDY 9.2

Circus Hub, Nottingham, series of weekend workshops, July 2018

Leaving behind more and more of these rule-bound playground games, today I wanted to use it. Why? It's a cold day and I wanted people to run around. It's a group with some new and some old people and I don't want to rush the new ones into the more structured laughter response too quickly as it might be too abstract for them. Nor do I want to take ages on that, repeating it for the old students.

The answer was the relatively new version of Grandmother's Footsteps with laughter conditioning. New details proliferated, such as:

LAUGHTER AS A PARDON

- If you are going back and we laugh, stay where you are to restart instead of going all the way back to the beginning.
- If we are laughing you can't be sent back – if you're going back already, stop at the point that we laugh.
- If we are laughing you can't win.
- If grandmother is looking at you, you can't advance.
- You can't advance when there is laughter.

This then made it much easier to 'pretend to play' the game – a version with no grandmother, where two, or even a solo, performers 'pretend' that they are playing the game. It's easier now, because you have the framework of the audience's laughter upon which to 'lean'. Rather than something abstract. You might:

- only advance if it's funny;
- risk advancing, if we laugh then keep going, if there's no laugh then go back;
- or just ignore all our responses!

Tips on being daring:

- Try and find the point where you get caught.
- Don't be afraid to be caught.
- Don't be afraid to be sent back.

When you've tried many variations of a game, you can ask yourself: 'what's my favourite way to play this game?' Competitively? Cheating? Losing? Absently?

10
CONCLUSIONS TO PART ONE: RIGHT AND WRONG THINKING

We've now covered an ample set of exercises and routes into a number of related concepts and practices. These have mainly centred around conditioning ourselves to respond to our audience, to enable a kind of conversation where you, the clown, can choose, or plan, to do pretty much what you want, without rules, but always in response to the spectators' part in that conversation, which consists of laughing or not laughing.

The only obstacles to this conditioning are our habits and beliefs – habits born of coping strategies, anxiety, fear, pride, low self-esteem – beliefs born of learning which we have undergone, especially any that mystifies performing, theatre and clowning, that clowns should or shouldn't be or do x, y or z, that clowning is the same as improvisation, that clowning is a, b, c, etc.

Why don't you hear the laughter?

Because you are engaged in:

- what you are doing;
- what you are feeling;
- how you think others see you.

But when you disengage from yourself, you are actually freer to engage with others (the audience) on terms that they can also freely participate in.

What will not change after this conditioning?

You still won't know:

- why they started laughing;
- why they stopped laughing.

But it doesn't matter!

What will you know about, after this conditioning?

- That they laughed.
- That they didn't laugh.

It's that simple. There are other things you will learn, some of which have come up already. Such as how you feel. We will deal with that in detail in the next part.

But, for now, prioritize 'doing the job' of observing and responding accurately to the laughs and silences, not the quality or quantity of the laughs/silences, not whether you expected or did not expect them. Whilst 'doing this job' you can do other things to keep yourself amused, but these will not disturb your observations.

This might be a radically new way of thinking for you, or feel very familiar. No matter. It is a way of thinking that will help you clown. Rather than obstruct or mystify your process. That's why it's logical to refer to this as 'right thinking'. It's fit for purpose, it's not a moral judgement, clearly.

A note on failure

We commonly associate failure, via the flop, with clowning. On the one hand, it denotes low status, lack of success in the social sense, whether that be physical failure, communication failure, or failure to understand. On the other hand, when as spectators we witness someone (on-or offstage) fail to achieve what we assume to be their goal, then we take it as symbolic proof that this moment of failure is 'true'. Our assumption is that failure is never willingly 'faked', and in this way it stands for 'authenticity', or lack of falsity. But what of the clown? We do expect failure from a clown, it is an almost defining characteristic that we are on the look-out for. Failure in a clown is a kind of success, a success in being a clown.

CONCLUSIONS TO PART ONE: RIGHT AND WRONG THINKING 129

But does this presentation of failure mean authenticity? This is a logical knot that much contemporary clowning has tied itself in. The knot comes about in the following way. Firstly, we observe that, in our general interactions, failure and showing that you are not successful (in other words vulnerability in front of others) convinces others that we are being genuine. But then, secondly, since clowns are 'conventionally' failures, suddenly that authenticity seems to dissolve, it looks fake, apparently. This then leads us, thirdly, to think we require an extra level of failure 'proof'. This comes about, supposedly, in the flop, the failure to be funny, which then becomes a different kind of 'funny'. In some ways, this extra demand, this double authenticity, can be a burden, both on those learning clowning and those practising it professionally. And on those teaching it, I might add.

This confidence that, symbolically, failure equals the real, the spontaneous, the live, is so well rooted that it crops up in non-clown performance, too. In some forms of theatre, failure is deliberately produced in order to, presumably, give the audience an experience of liveness. This happens across many styles, from old-fashioned English pantomime actors deliberately 'corpsing', to the more intellectual pursuits of the 'theatre of failure'.[1]

The current book doesn't really centre itself on any of this. Yes, there is an assumption that the flop is a useful tool, or route, towards learning clowning. But the emphasis here is on another kind of liveness, that of the conversation between stage and auditorium. When performers respond to audiences in the way explored here, a different kind of excitement opens up. A spectator might not laugh when they are 'supposed to'. Perceiving that they are being taken account of, an audience may become more active, talk back, or even start to 'perform itself', in recognition that it is being invited into a role. (Again, the English panto has its stock 'behind you' and boos on cue. And the genre of stand-up comedy often invites and welcomes the heckler.) Some child spectators of clowns might even try and take over the stage, or engage physically with clowns (yes, I'm talking about kids grabbing and kicking clowns here!). This kind of liveness is not one which is merely perceived in the dark of an otherwise fourth-walled[2] theatre, it is one which is co-created between performers and spectators.[3]

PART TWO

'I FEEL FUNNY'

Although the concern so far has been on directing our conscious decisions, on re-conditioning otherwise habitual and unconscious behaviour, by means of attention to laughter responses, we have already come across the obvious fact that this process, including the mere act of being in front of an audience, gives rise to feelings in the performer. Until now we have been concerned mostly with how you, as a performer, respond to your audience's responses – responses which you, from the stage, do not directly control, but can decide how to respond to. We will now explore how you respond through your own feelings – both in relation to the general situation of performing clown, and to those audience responses, too. What we are looking at here, then, are not conditionable responses (such as 'take a step') under the control of your conscious mind, but instead those emotional responses ('oh shit, no-one is laughing') that seem to arise whether you want them or not, and which appear outside of your control.

This may seem like a very dualistic approach, but in reality, the separation between the so-called conscious and the so-called unconscious is mixed up. But for now we will separate them out, just for the sake of focusing on one thing at a time in each exercise.

In Part One the job has been to attend to others' responses, not to your own. But any worker knows, whether their task is to refill supermarket shelves, apprehend criminals, or clinch international trade deals, that no matter how good you are at your job, you will have feelings whilst performing these tasks. The same goes for performers, obviously. We are familiar with the idea that actors have strong onstage emotions that have nothing to do with their professed tasks of creating characters, or telling stories. These emotions tend to be stage fright or elation.

Earlier, we glimpsed how the actual lived emotions of the performer in front of an audience are 'urgent' components of performance, whether it be scripted or improvised. We saw how Konijn's insights can help us understand clowning in particular, which may be seen as a kind of bare 'acting per se' (Konijn 1997: 108).

In the next section we will look at ways of exploring and becoming more aware of how our task emotions operate when clowning. These may be the typically identified ones:

> It was established that actors experienced a very specific range of emotions, including challenge, tension, and excitement, which I have called task-emotions. [. . .] Likewise, pleasure and tenderness were cited relatively frequently as actors' emotions.
>
> KONIJN 1997: 150

Or they may be very individually specific. It does not matter, as we will use the exercises to address whatever does come up as a 'feeling' for any given student. These will be anything you feel in the process of clowning, including learning and performing 'professionally', although the feelings may well differ in each context:

> The actors' task-emotions are activated during performance because the acting situation addresses concerns relevant to their profession. The **threat** to, or **satisfaction** of, at least four relevant concerns – competence, self-image, sensation seeking, and aesthetic concerns – hangs in the balance (chapter four).
>
> KONIJN 1997: 154

Konijn's claim, having examined what actors report about their task emotions and character emotions, was that performers' own task emotions are much stronger and intense than the fictional ones they habitually aim to create in portraying characters. Furthermore, she claimed to show that good actors transform their own task/stage feeling into the fictional ones in order to make the latter fuller and more powerful

'I FEEL FUNNY'

and hence more compelling and convincing for audiences. That, in a nutshell, is what acting is all about. Clowns, however, don't have so much fictional creativity to do. Clown scripts are simple, the roles are basic. Additionally, audiences don't expect clowns to convincingly impersonate others. Instead, it seems that they expect clowns to be convincing in other ways. To be convincingly 'themselves'. Whether this staged clown is the 'inner person', the 'real person', the 'clown persona', the 'person of the clown' or any other combination of those concepts, need not concern us too much here. What we do need to do, though, is address how to work without a character, in the actor's conventional sense. What happens to you when you are onstage, or, to put it another way around, when you 'stage yourself'? In order to face this task, we most certainly need ways to navigate our stage emotions when engaging in this task called clowning.

These subjective experiences and feelings are often at the forefront when we look at non-character comic performance, including both clowning and stand-up comedy (though not, perhaps, the comic characters required in comic plays, sketch comedy or even comedy improvisation). Everything we have heard over the past 60 years about contemporary clowns, at least in their training, has emphasized how the task – of standing up in front of everyone and making them laugh – is a monumental task. This task, essentially public speaking without a script, brings about feelings perceived negatively, of embarrassment, feeling shit, inadequate, boring, wanting to be swallowed up. 'I died onstage' say comedians. Different teachers may have different styles but the assumption is the same, that you will be funny when you come to terms with your own self-negativity. Gaulier will send you away in seconds, whilst others seek to teach *via positiva* (Sue Morrison,[1] for example), but the principle is the same.

This doesn't mean that this 'being in the shit' is the be-all-and-end-all of the matter, though. We can accept that the subjective experience is almost inevitable at the start, but that it is only a step. Once you are on good terms with your shit, let's say, it becomes less important. The laughter response conditioning tries to do both jobs at once. On the one hand, to point your attention towards your feelings of negativity, and on the other, to lead you away from an attachment to those feelings, away from self-obsession and ego, and placing your attention onto the audience. This is a relief.

And yet, once your attention has become a little detached from yourself and connected back to others out there in the world, your feelings still remain. How could they not? The instruction to not feel would be as absurd as the instruction not to think. We will always be alive in mind and heart, thinking, feeling, breathing, living. What counts is how much weight of attention you give to those thoughts and feelings. If you try to suppress thinking or feeling, you will either become hard, or you will fail and be in a state of constant self-punishment and self-obsession. Better to just accept that that is maybe how humans are, then live with the thoughts and feelings. Earlier on, I drew attention to thinking. Right and wrong thinking. Where to place your attention, with what to be concerned. Now let us deal with feelings in a parallel way.

11
I (DON'T) FEEL FUNNY

The first set of exercises recycles some of the patterns we've already used, but attach different responses to condition your awareness of feeling in response to your own actions and those of your spectators.

This begins in a way that parallels the previous 'that was/n't funny':

11.1 I caught the ball

- All throw and catch a ball in a circle.
- When you receive the ball, say what you did when catching (or failing to catch) the ball.

For example, beginning your speech with 'I caught the ball . . .', you might continue by adding:

- . . . with my left hand raised;
- . . . with both hands between my knees;
- . . . in front of my face;
- . . . stretching further than I wanted to.

If you fail to catch the ball, it might go something like this:

- I touched the ball with my right hand while jumping and it flew past.
- I reached down too far away from the ball.

136 THE CLOWNING WORKBOOK

11.1.1 . . . and I feel . . .

Now add an optional phrase describing how you feel in the moment you received the ball (if you don't know how to describe the feeling, just say what happened physically).

Something like: 'I caught the ball [with x] and I feel elated.' Or clever, or angry, or whatever feeling arises.

11.1.2 'I feel . . .'

Now say more about your feeling and say that first, adding any objective physical descriptions afterwards if you want to, as in:

- I feel powerful and I caught the ball without looking.
- I feel silly . . .
- I feel bored, I caught the ball easily again.

11.1.3 'I feel good/bad'

- Now approximate, if possible, your feeling description to 'I feel good' or 'I feel bad'. Often, we not only feel an emotion, but also at the same time make a value judgement about that feeling, regarding it as a 'positive' or a 'negative' emotion, something we want to feel or do not want to feel.

- This part of the exercise asks you to admit and declare how you feel about how you are feeling.

- If you can't be sure which side of the line your feeling is, just describe the feeling anyway.

11.1.4 'I feel funny' / 'I don't feel funny'

- Now choose one of these two phrases to describe your feeling (when possible).
- You might at any time change what you feel during the few seconds the spotlight is on you, by the way.

I (DON'T) FEEL FUNNY

- This might well be provoked by the act of saying what you feel, especially when it comes to saying the word 'funny'.

11.1.5 'I feel stupid'

- Now add a third option to the previous two (funny/not funny), which is 'I feel stupid'.
- Sometimes you might not distinguish between feeling stupid and feeling funny, or between feeling stupid and not feeling funny.
- 'Stupid' acts as both negative and positive in the clown context.

11.1.6 'I feel funny/stupid' for an audience

- Using the final version (three options of funny, not funny, or stupid), three people play throw and catch for an audience.

11.2 Free scripts

- Now we go back to the circle, but dispense with the 'script' of throwing and catching a ball.
- Anyone can do any (short) action, and must then say how they feel (funny, not funny, or stupid).

11.2.1 Free scripts for an audience

- Three people play the last version for an audience, each doing actions (if in doubt, do them one at a time) and saying how they feel.

11.2.2 Devised scripts

- Now decide what actions you are going to do before beginning the exercise.

- Three people spend a few minutes together agreeing an action they will do.
- They perform their action only when they feel funny, for an audience.
- Try the same but as a solo performer.
- When you don't feel funny, don't do your scripted action.
- When you don't feel funny, you can do any other, unscripted action.

This is just a taster for how we can work with pre-devised scripts. We will look at these possibilities in more detail in Part Three of this book.

11.3 'This is going to be funny'

- Back to the circle, and now you have an option to add the phrase 'This is going to be funny'.

This is the same exercise as 7.5 earlier, but it's worth repeating here in the new context.
Remember:

- Only say it when you actually do feel this, just as you are about to do your action.
- Don't use it as a rhetorical device to make us laugh through irony.
- No lying. Cheating in clowning can be fun and productive, but generally when the feelings are clear.
- Then say whether it was funny or not after doing it. It might coincide or not, it doesn't matter as long as your feeling was there before doing the action.
- Then in threes for an end-on audience.
- Back to the circle, with free actions, but **only** do them when you already feel stupid/funny (and can say 'this is going to be funny').
- Then in threes for an audience.

I (DON'T) FEEL FUNNY

At some point in these variations, you could find you don't need to say the phrases anymore, once you've conditioned yourselves to be accurate and honest about how you feel. If you are still unclear about what you feel and when, then keep saying the phrases.

11.4 Homework

You can actually practise this in your spare time or daily routines!

- Practise spotting when you feel stupid. Once you've set yourself the task, you'll be surprised how easy it becomes to spot.
- Keep a 'I feel stupid' journal. Note down when you felt stupid, what was happening, what seemed to provoke the feeling, or how you reacted.

This is simply another tool for the conditioning we are exploring. In every job there are certain things you will be expected to look out for, pay attention to and spot. For example, a traffic warden looks for cars parked wrongly, a plumber for leaks, etc. If you have an eye for these things you would probably be good at those jobs.

- Revisit some of the previous exercises but now exploring how you feel.
- Seek out your stupidity.

In Name Tag, for example, we encountered the fear (a key negative feeling) of losing habitually which often pushes us to retreat and not to look into the eye of the tagger (aggressor), nor of the audience, for fear of losing. These are, as we have seen, wrong ways of thinking for clowning. If we now welcome that negative feeling of fear as potentially one which will lead us to be ridiculous, and feel stupid/funny, then we might even seek it out.

- Look people in the eye.

The instruction, 'when you are in danger, look at the audience and move forwards, towards us' becomes a way to embrace the feeling. In fact, looking at the audience is one of the single biggest things one can do in order to induce an emotion in the context of performance. In clowning it will induce strong feelings of fear, embarrassment, etc.

- What happens when we look at the audience?

We are these days accustomed to clown teachers demanding that we 'look at the audience!' and this is normally explained or theorized as being in order for the audience to be able to read the feelings and thoughts of the clown. but what if we thought of this mechanism the other way around. What if looking at the audience served principally to ignite [negative] feelings in the clown performer? Since, when I look at the audience, I see their response to me, they judge me, am I funny or not? This judgement then provokes my own feelings, which, when witnessed by the audience, provoke new responses in them. It's a conversation, a dynamic one, where each (spectators and clowns) provokes each other's next feeling.[1]

- If the looking at the audience evokes instant feelings, then so too does looking at your clown partner, or, if you are practising outside of a class, anyone who is with you. When you look at them, what do you feel? Who is this person?

Feeling, speaking, acting – which comes first?
With these exercises we can experience several permutations. Feeling, doing (moving), (the act of) speaking, thought, clearly all affect and trigger each other. Although we probably get what actor trainers mean when they have said such things as 'feel, then speak',[2] or 'move, then feel',[3] this trying to establish an axiomatic rule is empirically absurd, and certainly unnecessary.

With these exercises, then, try all combinations:

- Move and act first, then check how you feel having done it.

This is the basic first phase of the exercise, testing what you feel once you've done something.

I (DON'T) FEEL FUNNY

- If you don't feel, don't act.

This is the strict version of conditioning, only allowing yourself action when the stupid or funny feeling is present.

- Speak first, saying 'How do I feel?' aloud, then check what feeling emerges.

Hearing the question may well provoke a feeling response in you, it might even be 'I feel stupid'! The act of asking is as good an action as any designed to elicit a feeling response.

CASE STUDY 11.1

Week workshop, AFDA, Johannesburg, April 2018

AC This is going to be funny.

Jon Does anyone else agree with me. It's not. [I mean that we can't sense AC's feeling this for real.]

ALL Agreed.

Jon The fact is that I don't believe you.

SJ You're hoping.

Jon Don't hope, tell the truth. About your subjective feeling.

AC This is going to be funny.

Jon I don't believe you.

AC shouts it. I'm not convinced.

Jon You can do actions without this feeling, or with it. The actor doesn't always feel something. But the actor must always do something. After the action comes the judgement. And the judgement could be yes or no, in both cases, whether you felt something before or not. I don't think you felt it was going to funny. I think you thought it was, or thought it should be, funny. Or hoped it would be.

The influence of improv comedy

(In this group there were a number of experienced improv comedy performers.)

The self-motivating credo of improv might have something to answer for here. Comics use adrenaline to boost confidence. As a clown, this is your enemy, as it works to build a fragile ego that hopes and desires to be successful and that has no way of processing positively any failure to be funny. Luckily, as clowns, we have a built-in way to absorb failure. It is part of what makes us clowns.

Actions only when you feel funny

Jon For the moment still say 'this is going to be funny'. If you don't feel that, don't do anything. No lying! Liars! Then you comment after.

KD So we're adding another layer?

Jon Well, we're removing a lot of layers.

Tip for student: if you are already feeling funny, i.e. you are laughing at what has just been happening, then chances are, if you do something when still in that state, while still laughing, that whatever you do will be funny, because it will be driven by your 'finding things funny'.

We don't care if it was funny or not. Or who does what. Just be truthful. Even if something was funny, but you don't feel funny, you can't do it.

Jon Do you feel funny?

CC No.

Jon You look like you do feel funny.

CC I don't.

Everyone laughs.

CC I do now.

Jon So you can do anything you want!

CC Anything?

I (DON'T) FEEL FUNNY   143

We laugh.

Jon   Still feel funny, right?

CC's feeling overwhelms her. We know we love her like this, but she isn't convinced. She is a natural clown but isn't sure.

Jon   When you realize that we like you like this, you might change your perspective on yourself. Know what I'm saying?

CC   Yes. It's scary.

Jon   Yes, I know. It's a process. We'll turn the scary into fun.

AC   I don't think I can be funny like this. It's too real.

She cries.

Jon   I'll go with you.

I hold her hand as she tries to restart the exercise. AC wants to try, but it's difficult. She is feeling 'too much'. I sense that she's been avoiding feeling things, especially bad things. There might be a way through for her here. Another person in her group has loads of jokes. I ask AC to do LI's joke, only when AC feels funny, speaking when you feel funny.

LI   Knock, knock.

AC   Who's there?

AC cries. We laugh.

LI   Adam.

AC   Adam who?

[The 'act' dissolves into laughter.]

Jon   Another one. I have a joke for you, tell this one (I whisper it to AC).

AC   What's brown and sticky?

She is laughing. We laugh. She bows.

144   THE CLOWNING WORKBOOK

Jon   We've done earlier in the week, doing things when others laugh, when you laugh. Or when we think we know when you're lying about how you feel.

Do you see the difference?

AC   I'm so confused. Clowns are real and not real?

Jon   But telling the joke isn't honest. I even told you what to say. There's nothing authentic there. But your feeling is real. There's a mixture of the real, the true, and the stupid joke which has no truth.

Jon (to LI)   This is your new career. You present yourself as cool, but then you crack up with your own jokes before you finish. It was very surprising.

Jon   You CAN do things when you don't feel funny, but be careful.

KD   So if you're onstage what do you do, stand there when you don't feel funny?

Jon   It's just a training exercise. It's a good idea to feel funny. Can you cultivate it? It fits with clowning. You don't have to do all the things we're doing on the course. It's just advice. It's not fool proof.

X   Is clowning informed by your own personality?

Jon   I think we see that here, how each person has a different way.

That doesn't mean that each person re-invents clowning rules for themselves. Clowning has a general definition but each person will execute it in a distinct manner.

Equally, an actor will do a role in their individual way. But the role is still Hamlet.

Clowning is something we all potentially have. At least informally, in a social context.

You might also find that you prefer to clown in a particular situation: for kids, for adults, in commercial shop openings, in restaurants, one to one in the street, in a theatre, in a comedy club.

CASE STUDY 11.2

Week workshop, Brussels, July 2019

During the initial stages of this five-day workshop there was some general awareness about the usefulness of the mechanics of the conditioning explored (the first part of this book), but some students assumed it was not addressing the issue they were used to encountering in clown training, namely the emotions.

However, once we moved onto Feeling Exercises on day three, perspectives shifted radically. Plus, on day five using the mirror (see next section here), we saw what a powerful tool it was for contacting all those dark, negative feelings, shame, or guilt, that plague clown training. This clarified somewhat where feeling exercises fit into what looks initially like a mechanical 'system'.[4]

Such a framework is based on the assumption that clowning happens as a dynamic relationship or conversation between clown and spectator, mentioned already.

Testing

- The point of actions (in this exercise) is to TEST how you feel.

- The actions are NOT there to entertain us, be creative, or impress us, or even to be funny.

- Remember: this is just an exercise. It does NOT replicate everything you will find in a real, live performance. Its intention is to practise awareness of stage feeling, in relation to our performing and our audience.

- This applies to both the 'free' (improvised) actions and to the prepared (scripted) actions. The difference is that with the planned actions you aren't concerned about wondering what to do, and so you may attend more easily to your responses.

146   THE CLOWNING WORKBOOK

Action/reaction

Action (clown's choice)
Reaction (clown's feeling)
Your feeling-reaction might be activated by:

- a. your actioning/acting/act/action;
- b. what you perceive spectator's reactions (feelings) to be;
- c. spectator's laughter/silence reaction;
- d. you merely being onstage in front of an audience.

Take your time to spot or identify your feeling.

- If you identify your feeling while acting, stop the action, since it's served its purpose, which is to test/provoke/activate your feeling reaction.

Some feelings come/arise as you act.
Some feelings arise before/as you are about to act.
Some feelings arise after you act, immediately or delayed.

In 'real life' you can have a strong feeling ('oh, what an idiot I am!') as you are doing something, or just after you leave the situation, or in anticipation of something.

CASE STUDY 11.3

Weekly clown course, London Clown School, January 2020

On feeling shit or not knowing what you feel

In some clown circles, 'being in the shit' has become a tagline to indicate the best place from which clowning can emerge (as well as being a marker which indicates within which school of clown training the speaker places themselves). As ever, in the context of performer training, the choices of words will generally be pretty specific to the actual, real-time context being shared by those present. Our attempts to describe what's going on in workshops are always specific to the actual practice. When we go further and extrapolate general deductions or conclusions, the words chosen remain the same, but travel to other times and places (and languages) and so easily get re-interpreted, according to whichever new specific context they happen to find themselves in.[5]

For example, a student feels angry at the audience's blank reaction. The student wants to be loved. What side does anger go in? Bad. Not funny. I don't feel funny.

VA   I feel I'm not doing the exercise right.

Jon   OK, herd it. Not funny? So this feeling of being bad becomes useful. By being identified according to clown options.

Practise this 'herding' of feelings into one 'pen' or another (funny, not funny).

It's important to have the three options. Just having a binary choice risks just deciding without reflecting.

Important note: the aim of this exercise is not to get really good at being able to identify every feeling you have. That way lies misery as you will end up punishing yourself for not knowing what you feel sometimes. No, the aim is to be able to herd the feelings into useful pens. So all the unidentifiable feelings, all the shame, all the crap, has somewhere to go. It goes in the pen marked 'I don't feel funny'.

One day, a class[6] had an in-joke about diarrhoea, something about someone throwing a handful of warm shit at someone. I don't know if it was fictional or real or what, but it was very amusing for them. As we worked through the feeling exercises over the course of our weekly three-hour session, the joke became useful. The conclusion being, that you have to have somewhere to shit. To leave your shit. To go to when you're shit. In previous exercises we've seen the same principle: if you're not funny, you leave, for example. This isn't a negative once you realize that on/off, funny/not, are binaries that function to produce clowning. Wanting to be funny always is just like wanting never to shit (that's painful and impossible) or to live for ever. It won't happen.

Figure 7: I Feel Funny: Jon Davison.

12
SELF-LAUGHTER

The initial exercise that is the foundation of this section came to my notice in a curious book aimed at boosting company productivity by using laughter techniques, in which the source was cited as a Buddhist monk who explained the spiritual value of self-laughter.[1] I won't detain you here in discussions on spirituality and capitalism but will get to the point and summarize the phases of the exercise and look at how it fits into the broader 'system' of laughter response. I will also draw on some case studies that reveal potential obstacles. (This is another of the handful of exercises in this book that I have explored in detail in previous writings.[2])

12.1 Basic mirror self-laughter – solo

- One person sits on a chair facing directly a mirror placed so they can see their face and (ideally) whole body.
- The person is in profile to the audience.
- There are only two rules:
    1. You must laugh constantly, no long pauses, just for normal breaths.
    2. You can only look at your reflection in the mirror or at the audience (not at the floor, ceiling, or above people's heads.
- Laughter can be 'real' (involuntary) or 'fake' (voluntary).
- Avoid 'actor's laughter', i.e. any really good imitation of real laughter – we want it to be clear when it's real and when it's fake.
- Spend a few minutes per person.

The aim of the exercise is not, as many assume, to attain as much real laughter as possible. The initial aim is to follow the rules of the exercise and treat the real and the fake as equals. And to control where you look. This resembles other exercises we have already looked at, where the aim is not to get as many audience laughs as possible, but to be accurate.

12.1.1 Basic mirror laughter – duos

- Two people do the exercise at the same time.
- One sits in the chair as before, one stands as close as they can to the chair, so they are in the same space.
- Both must laugh constantly, as before.
- You now have three places you can look: your reflection, the audience, or your partner.

12.1.2 Mirror laughter plus conditioned action

- Returning to a single participant, this time you must stand up from the chair whenever your laughter is real/involuntary.
- Remain standing as long as you are laughing for real.
- Sit down as soon as the laughter switches to fake.

Not only does this clarify when you are laughing for real or not (both for you and for spectators), but also the actions of standing and sitting will have an effect on your laughter. You can substitute other predetermined actions for the standing up if you wish, like raising your arm. But standing will have the biggest effect.

- Now do the standing/sitting version with two people at once, each of them with their own chair.
- If you are getting along well with this, try pointing the chairs to face the audience and dispense with looking in the mirror.

SELF-LAUGHTER

12.2 Mirror laughter plus free action

- Now when you stand on laughing for real, also do some kind of action.
- The action should last the same time as the real laugh, being done simultaneously.
- When the laugh becomes fake, stop the action and sit down.
- Try this solo, in pairs, and also in a group of three.
- If you can't think of any action to do, just walk around the chair.
- If you want, you can try this without the chairs, beginning standing and waiting for the real laugh to trigger your action.

12.2.1 Mirror laughter plus planned action

- As above, but now you will have planned, or be given by someone, a specific action to perform whenever you laugh for real.
- Any action that can actually be done (not mimed) will work, such as: marching, dancing, fighting, sneezing, falling over, singing, and so on.

12.2.2 Silence and real laughter

- Finally, try being silent instead of doing the fake laughter.
- Now we have either silence and no action OR real laugh plus action.

What use is the fake?

As already seen, the obligation to do something or speak something (whether improvised or scripted) is a powerful stimulus for eliciting responses (from your audience and from yourself). The responses which interest us here are laughter (and its absence) but also any feeling you

152 THE CLOWNING WORKBOOK

may experience as a performer in the moment of being in front of an audience (which you may judge as negative or positive).

The fake laugh (which in itself is rather ridiculous, given that we assume that laughter must normally be 'real' to count as laughter) frequently provokes quick responses. This powerful tool can really work in your favour, if you regard it as a tool for exploration.

Use the fake laugh to test how you feel.

- Try and modulate your fake laugh and bring it near to your actual feeling. Experiment with your voice, its pitch, intensity, timbre, and see if it might trigger a feeling for you.
- Approximate the manner of your fake laugh to match your actual feelings.
- Don't do theatre with the fake laugh.
- Make sure it's recognizable as a laugh, not an animal or singing, otherwise it won't have the right meaning and it won't make you feel stupid.
- When the real laugh happens and you are obliged to stand up and perform, it may be that you retain your negative feeling during this section whilst you laugh/perform.

CASE STUDY 12.1

Weekend workshop, Gent, Belgium, February 2018

Workshops which are open to anyone vary in their homogeneity, depending on location and other factors. Large or capital cities tend to produce more diverse mixtures of backgrounds, whilst smaller towns often draw participants from nearby who share language and culture. Gent is a small city in the northern Belgian region of Flanders, and on this occasion just one participant was not from the area.[3] This turned out to present us (as a group, including the students and myself as teacher) with some unexpected challenges, obstacles which turned out to be ideal critical points for learning.

First signs of a group response which was not what I was used to came on day one while doing some of the exercises from Part One of this book. For

SELF-LAUGHTER

example, while throwing and catching the ball, with actions conditioned to the presence of laughter:

Jon No one is laughing. Doesn't anyone feel ridiculous?

Group Hmm, sometimes.

Jon But you're not laughing?

Participant I am.

Jon I didn't hear it.

Participant I laugh on the inside.

Others nodding in agreement Yes, me too.

Overnight, I racked my brain for a way around what for me was an obstacle. If they weren't prone to laughing out loud, then how could my exercises which depend on laughter have any effect for them? Which exercise might be able to get round this issue?

The following day I decided to concentrate on the mirror laughing exercise and go through all its permutations if necessary. We began the morning, then, with the exercise phases as described in this section. It seemed that the exercise was indeed having an effect on many in the group, who seemed to be feeling stupid, laughing at themselves and/or enjoying watching their classmates do the exercise.

However, after the first few phases (before moving on to using improvised and predetermined actions), the feedback and observations revealed something different to my perceptions. I realized that my judgements as to what was real and what was fake laughter had been wildly inaccurate in many cases.

Taking a break from the routine of 'teacher proposes exercise, students do exercise', I confessed that I felt we were going backwards. The group agreed that we weren't understanding each other enough. Together we agreed that I would coach them in detail in the next exercises and point out whenever I felt they were going down a path I wasn't wanting them to take. This would mean me intervening continually in the exercises, rather than giving instructions and waiting to see how they responded.

I think we all felt relief and pleasure that we had overcome an obstacle and found a new way to progress. And progress we made. Until I realized that once again, the group had found a new way to take a different path. While working on the phase of trios performing pre-determined actions only when they laugh real (13.1.5 above), it became apparent that during the fake laugh periods they were also 'making theatre', as it were. Using the impossibility of communicating or acting as the basis for a play of looks, sounds, and micro-gestures which wanted to tell a kind of story of how difficult it was to make anything happen. This, in itself, is creative, undoubtedly. But it was also a way of negating the effect of the exercise: instead of being forced to 'not create' while no real laugh occurred, they were making sense out of what was supposed to be nothing. This meant that there was no contrast between the 'nothing' and the 'something'. We switched to the next phase (silence instead of fake laughs) but even here the urge was strong to make theatre out of silence.

What got learnt? Who can ever answer that question?! As a teacher, I am aware that students will not always learn what I think I am teaching them. Maybe they learn that they don't like clowning, or don't like me, or whatever! For me, though, the lesson was probably to become more attentive to that contrast, between the non-acting and the acting, and that somehow this was a key ingredient in clowning. Of course, the other, more obvious lesson, is that an exercise is only useful if it works for the students. If it doesn't work, then it's the exercise's fault, not theirs. And when, as a teacher, one visits another culture, country or community, beware the cultural divide and never assume that you are right. [4]

CASE STUDY 12.2

BA Theatre and Performance Practice, London Metropolitan University, November 2019

Despite my insistence on no actor-laughs, the first student gives a wonderful demonstration of fake, but convincing laughter. She enjoys it immensely, as do the audience. Hmmm, maybe the next one will crack. One after another, the same pattern emerges. I wonder if they have done 'laughing' in a voice class? Such that they have no feelings of fear or embarrassment on doing these fake

SELF-LAUGHTER 155

laughs. In fact, they appear to have no feelings of their own at all. But isn't that what an actor is? Someone who can imitate emotions and actions, without seeming to have their own feelings about that imitation? To be an expert without shame?

As we work through the class (some 16 people), we get to those who clearly weren't so confident about doing this, admittedly challenging exercise. Let's face it, it begins with solos in front of everyone. There is no game or work in groups preceding the individual experience. In the last half dozen students, there starts to be a hint of feelings. Of stupidity, of embarrassment, shame, anxiety. The final student is creased up with embarrassment. Their fake laughs are so terribly unconvincing that everyone is in hilarious waves of laughter.

I ask: what elements are there here? Real, fake, and emotions? They observe correctly that sometimes it's the fake laughter that makes you laugh for real since you feel stupid. I ask whether we saw everyone's feelings. No, they observe, correctly.

Next, in pairs. Although this exercise is NOT about achieving real laughs, I would say it IS about exposing real feelings about your fake or real laughs. Once they have a friend to work with, this group of young students take off. Looking at each other sends them into hysterics. In only one single case is there no real laughter in a pair.

Planned actions. The plans, often theatrical (they are studying acting!) and often drawing on their other assignments or classes, or just in-jokes, end up trashed by the hysterics. Marvellous!

CASE STUDY 12.3

MA Voice Studies, RCSSD, London, May 2018

Laughter has a unique place as part of our vocal repertoire. Although we sometimes talk about 'silent laughter' or 'laughing on the inside', audible laughter (for the hearing) seems to claim a special place for itself as a phenomenon. One could expect laughter to play a major role in voice training, and it is true up to a point that the particularities of saccadic breathing (the breathing involved in both laughing and crying) will certainly be familiar to those in that field. However, as far as I am aware, the exploration of laughter in voice studies is less common from a psycho-emotional point of view, and much less so within the framework that this book is concerned with, in examining how we behave onstage in front of audiences. The opportunity to work over several days with students specializing in voice evidenced obvious and immediate connections.

Some students find it difficult to distinguish between their own (or others') real and fake laughter. Or at least, their execution of the exercise seems to indicate this. Sometimes it's a question of attention, or lack of it. Perhaps the attention is placed on wanting to produce something real, or wanting to sound good, or be a good actor. All these concerns can usefully be dumped, as far as we can manage that. Interestingly, it seemed that voice students didn't experience this differently to non-specialists. When asked to move only on real laughter, it was not always easy to know if a moving student was in fact laughing 'for real'.

Jon   What did you notice?

LP   As the person doing the exercise, surprisingly little amount of that was real. Most things fake. And I thought I would get to real.

Jon   Don't worry about that.

LP   I'm not worried.

Jon   When you actually have to not do anything when it's fake, maybe that's when you notice it. It also helps us to notice it. The more you distinguish between the two [fake/real], the more pleasure, the more playful it's going to be. What else?

HS   For me it was the opposite. Because the physical motion of laughing would just induce real laughter. And then it came to a point where it physically hurt and it wouldn't stop. So that was interesting.

Jon   Yes, it's hard work. Anything else you noticed while watching them?

Student   It was interesting when you introduce the movement, move when you're really laughing. Because there were moments when L was moving, and I was, like, is she laughing? It was really interesting to note whether or not that was real. Similarly, with H, I felt some of her laughter was real, but she was still.

SELF-LAUGHTER

I ask the students if they know anything about body posture and positions during laughter. Do the voice students know of physiological explanations or descriptions of laughter? They speak about contractions and exhaustion. We mostly recognize the position of a body collapsing while laughing.

But what happens when you open your body consciously in that moment? What symbolic or other meaning might it have? Why did it not appear in textbooks on posture? These works did often show diagrams of 'bad' posture, often drawing parallels with emotional states – but why not laughter?[5]

Another pair try the exercise, they appear to be more accurate in differentiating between real and fake laughs. But is the trained voice an obstacle to feeling stupid when you fake-laugh?

Expanding on the exercise a little, we next try and convert the real laughter into something else, not a movement while laughing as previously, but another sound.

Another pair does the exercise.

Jon   OK, what did you notice?

Student   Reluctant to leave the anchor [fake] laugh that they had.

Jon   Yes, so your fake laugh was very solid, wasn't it? Let's see what happens if you open up, let's try to open up that fake laugh, so it's not a block. So it's a little bit like when we were playing before with the ball – if I throw the ball, my job is to elicit a response. Try to use your fake moment to elicit a response rather than to stimulate yourself. Because if we get too far in that we end up with too much fake stuff. Let's open that up. So when you're doing your fake laugh, try to use that moment of fake to try to tease out something else, of yourself or the other or of the audience.

Three people try the exercise.

Jon   What do you notice?

Student   I did see moments, of one movement being infectious, drawing in one of them. It was never all three doing it at the same time.

Jon   From the clown point of view, perhaps from a dramatic point of view, it's good when we're not caught doing the same thing. Why would we have three actors doing the same thing? We could employ one to do the same thing? Why

158 THE CLOWNING WORKBOOK

pay for three? So we've got three actors, we want different things. So you find yourself going 'oh, it's gone, no laughter, nothing', while the other two are having a great time – that's a good thing. Because that's what we want. It's more interesting to see extreme contrast.

Jon   Again, I would emphasize, whilst the sound, or the movement, or those words, or the facial expression, or whatever is out there, it is something not just for us [the audience] to respond to, but for you [the performer] to respond to. So you respond to yourself, you respond to others, we respond. It's a multi dynamic thing. That's also why the flop is a good thing, because that's another thing you can respond to. When we had some flops in the circle, we had responses to them. It's good. Sometimes the response to the flop is that, 'oh, there's no response'. The response is to the lack of response – that's a good response.

Another trio does the exercise but now with silence instead of fake laughter.

Jon   All of this plus there must be a word, at least one, when it's involuntary laughter. Plus, sometimes those words will be not your own words. Words that have been written or spoken, that you have heard? So you're not thinking 'Oh, where's this word coming from?' It could be from a play or what your mother said to you this morning or what you ordered in the cafe or something already said.

Jon   What's the effect of words? It seemed like there was a shift in responses to yourself speaking words, and to others.

Student   What I mostly observed was when they needed to think of a word that they went into, have to think of words.

Jon   Yeah, that was one response.

Student   But also when they said the word, another person would get more contagious.

Jon   But they have a different kind of effect to all the other stuff.

SELF-LAUGHTER 159

Where are we up to now?

We have now covered responding/acting/not acting when:

a. others laugh [Step-Laugh, etc.];

b. you feel stupid/funny;

c. you laugh (mirror).

These three might all coincide in the same moment, but they might not, depending on what kind of person or clown you are and what kind of audience you have. So you have three options, three chances to go forward.

Now let's practise all three:

- Half the class line up against the back wall, and walk straight towards the other half who are sitting as audience facing them.

- Only step forward whenever you think we have laughed at you, or you laugh, or you feel stupid.

- When you get to us, turn around and go back. And so on. Stay in your lane.

This is actually just a return to Gaulier's exercise, slightly more elaborated. Which is where this evolution probably began, even though when I was developing my exercise, I didn't remember Gaulier's version at all (thanks to Lucy Amsden for reminding me).

Figure 8 Mirror Laugh: Camille Suarez.

13
READING OTHERS' FEELINGS

Once you become accustomed to identifying your own feelings that arise while performing, it doesn't feel like such a big step to begin reading others' feelings. Although there is a clear difference: your experience of your own feelings is an immediate knowledge; whereas your reading of others can only ever be an interpretation.

This section is about some simple ways of training our attention onto wondering what the other feels. It is a good preparation for the following section which presents a potentially familiar exercise (modified for clowning) which involves more complex processes. Sometimes there is the need for a more extensive set of varied exercises. In the larger sized groups of around 15 people, the process of everyone doing an exercise in threes, pairs or solo gives the whole class plenty of examples and time to learn and reflect on what the exercise can teach you. In a smaller group, though, there will be fewer examples and less time spent on any one exercise. Obviously, you can repeat the exercise more times, but it is sometimes a good idea to explore some of the themes of an exercise one by one.

That was the origin of the following set of exercises in one of my classes, as a lead-in to the 'Guess the Show' (next section).

13.1 Doing the expected

- Throw and catch the ball, in a circle.
- Throw it in ways that the receiver does not expect.
- Throw in exactly the way the receiver expects.

Teaching note: we are very used to training ourselves in exploring the unexpected in clowning, since producing the unexpected is exactly what clowns are . . . expected to do!

But what if we explored its opposite as well?

When doing the expected, your attention shifts entirely from yourself and onto the receiver (because the 'expected' stems from the other, not yourself). Your own desires, ideas, preferences or habits should dissolve and you become the servant of another. But deliberately, consciously. No initiative! No ego!

13.1.1 Doing the expected for an audience

Next, move from circle to audience:

- Three people throw and catch the ball, the thrower always fulfilling the receiver's expectations, while all three divide their eye contact between themselves and the audience 50/50.

Teaching note: in this format it may become clearer that the receivers must have a certain initiative, or do something in order for the thrower to perceive what they expect. But make sure that anyone doing any of these actions or initiatives only does them in order to elicit a response. So each person will have only two options:

1 Do something in order to elicit a response from someone.
2 Respond to someone.

That means there shouldn't be any examples of actions being one 'just because I felt like it'.

Next:

- Change the 'script' of throwing and catching the ball for some other activity.

- I like to put a couple of chairs and a table in the space for the three people to use, for example.

READING OTHERS' FEELINGS

Things to avoid:

- Don't do the thing you want another person to do. Do something that invites the other to complement your initiative, not to join in with it.
- Don't point to indicate what you want (act or speak if you need to).

13.2 Doing what the audience expects

Next, we shift the expectation from your fellow performers to the audience:

- In threes, do what the audience expects.

How on earth will we know what the audience expects? To simplify here, you can simply notice the audience reactions to what you do. Does the audience respond to your action by

- Rejecting it?
- Accepting it?

You will have to 'read' the audience here. One marker of their acceptance or rejection will of course be their laughter or their silence, as we have now become well accustomed to. But there will be other, less objective signals. What faces are they making? Bored? Disgusted? Open-mouthed? Excited?

You will also find that generally there will only be responses **after** you have first done something. It's a hard ask to expect an audience to respond to 'nothing'. (Similarly, we have seen how the flop is predicated on the 'feat', the attempt.)

First you act, then the audience respond, then you respond to that response. If they reject your action, don't do it anymore! If they accept, keep going!

14
GUESS THE SHOW

This is an exercise which I adapted to make it useful for clowning, from a common strain of exercises in other forms of performer training. In the latter, the audience indicates knowingly their approval of the performer is 'warm' by doing such things as raising their hand, clapping more or less intensely, and so on. In the version described here, the performer must read the audience's reactions 'as an audience'. The spectators do not have to 'add' anything to their responses, but just 'spectate'. I will suggest reasons for this once I have described the exercise below.

14.1 Solo performance

- One person leaves the room, or moves to wherever they cannot hear the others speaking.

- The others decide one thing they want the person to do onstage for them when they return.

- The person is called back and aims to do whatever it is has been decided, but with no knowledge or clues as to what that is.

- When the performer does exactly what had been decided for them, the audience applaud and the exercise is over.

Maybe because of the existence of the other versions mentioned above, the good use of this exercise generally needs a fair bit of extra guidance:

Reality
The thing decided by the audience must be something that the performer can actually do, or at least try to do. There is an infinite number of such things to choose from, for example:

THE CLOWNING WORKBOOK

- Sit on the floor.
- Shout 'help'.
- Dance (any style or a particular style).
- Jump.
- Pretend to sleep.
- Pretend to sneeze.
- Pretend to cry.
- Pretend to . . . anything else!.
- Sing a song (any song or a particular song or a particular style).
- Recite lines from Shakespeare.
- Leave the room.
- Shake hands with someone.
- Count to ten.
- Take tiny steps from upstage towards the audience.
- Switch off the lights.

You get the idea. You can choose simple or detailed, but always 'do-able'.

Avoid, on the other hand, anything that requires us to know, imagine or otherwise accept something that is not actually here and now, such as:

- Sail a boat to Antarctica.
- Be Henry VIII.
- Do the whole of *Hamlet*.

In other words, avoid fictional places and fictional times. And avoid the impossible or the impossibly abstract.[1]

Why? Because in order to place such fictions on the stage you will expend so much creative energy that it becomes an intellectual game of charades, rather than a performance of a clown before an audience.

Audience honesty

Contrary to the other exercises mentioned, here the audience is not required to behave in any way they would not do so in a normal performance. They watch, they listen, maybe they laugh, they yawn, their feelings appear on their facial expressions and body language as they sit (or not!). Asking an audience to do something mechanical to interpret their own response (like raise your hand if you like it) immediately changes their nature as an audience. Most importantly, it allows them to lie, to be polite. Which doesn't help us here, as we want to train ourselves in the art of reading the audience.[2]

Even applause when the performer is 'warm' feels contrived. But applause at the end when they have finally or magically achieved what they had no idea they were trying to achieve: that feels good!

14.2 Duo performance

- Now two people leave the room together.
- The rest decide on an action for them to do.
- They return and do it.

Just as, with one performer, our decisions should be things they can do here and now, so for two performers together. Plus, let us choose something that actually uses two people. Why have two people doing the same thing? That would be the same as the solo shows, but less fun. Again, there are numerous possible choices for two performers:

- Hug each other.
- One trips the other up.
- One kicks the other's bottom.
- One sings for the other to dance (general or particular style).
- They sing in harmony.
- They dance a specific couples dance (waltz, foxtrot, polka).
- One sits on the other's shoulders.

- One says 'I love you' and the other replies 'I don't'.
- One pretends to kill the other.

Ad infinitum . . .

This is a great chance to practise scripting for two. Remember Johnstone's 'don'ts'? Don't join in, don't do the same agreed activity. Look for drama.

14.3 Trio shows

The same principles apply for a three-person show. What kinds of choices can we make if we have three people at our disposal?

- Play a love triangle scene.
- One sings while two do a couple dance.
- One breaks up a fight between the other two.

14.4 Audience variations

If you really get into this exercise, you can invent new permutations, such as:

- Only one part of the audience knows/decides the show. The rest of the audience have no idea.
- Different parts of the audience make different choices for what they want the performer to do, and applaud accordingly.

Some other dos and don'ts

- Don't commentate, especially negatively, such as saying 'no it's not that'.
- Don't say the things you are doing, just do them.
- We are your brain. Look to us for clues.
- Don't discuss ideas with your stage partner(s), just act.

GUESS THE SHOW

- Being funny doesn't mean you are close, it just means it's funny.
- If you sense you are close, go into detail and try variations.

CASE STUDY 14.1

Week workshop, University of the Arts, Cape Town, February 2017

BN does the exercise. She enters the room through the door from the corridor and strides towards the centre, her head turned to look at us all the time. She moves hesitantly, her arms swinging slowly and stiffly, she is smiling, nearly laughing. It seems in anticipation of how this difficult task will make her appear silly. During the workshop she has had no resistance to this. Some spectators laugh with her. She stops in the centre and seems undecided whether to face forward or with her back to us. It seems she is testing both positions. She waves, but it seems pointless to do so. She does a simple dance, changing weight and clicking her fingers and half-heartedly humming. No reaction. She does a forward lunge. No reaction. She gestures with one hand moving from her chest towards us declaring 'if I speak like this . . .' in a voice too big for the space. No reaction. She laughs. Some spectators then laugh. She tries the same gesture and speech again but with a slightly different intonation. No reaction. She smiles and lifts her dress a little with both hands, seemingly unconsciously. She makes some sideways lunge movements and smiles, spectators laugh as well, seemingly at the odd movement. She pauses in position at these laughs, as if they might indicate she is close. But she isn't. She looks hopeful but puzzled. She tries making similar movements to what she thought we just laughed at. There are one or two laughs. She smiles and looks more lost. More laughs follow. She tries the same movement, there are some laughs, but probably because she is very wrong. She jumps straight up, it's a surprise, then repeats the move from before. She keeps looking hopeful. More laughs because of this. She tries a spin. She looks almost proud that she has done something new. No reaction. Then a laugh. She repeats, to more laughs. She is more hopeful, which brings more laughs. She repeats what she thinks we like, with more energy, but there is no reaction at all now. She wanders to her right and then approaches us. Strong laughs. She tries stepping closer, which provokes a single big laugh. She tries a small step, to see if we react. We are waiting. She gestures as if to apologize for encroaching on our space. Then does her movements from before but now in the middle of the audience. Laughs. She laughs even more, still with no clue. She makes a big lunge move suddenly addressed to one spectator, who laughs, as does she. She retreats a little towards the stage area, then returns to another part of the audience. She tries the same again to a new person, bringing some small laughs. There is a sound of something falling in another part of the room and she looks around, worried. Laughs. She walks back to the centre, efficiently now, frustrated, and turns to face us. She moves her arms up and down while looking at us constantly to check our reaction. Variations in the moving arms next. We are laughing intermittently at her attempts. Everything feels hopeless. She bends forwards, arms outstretched and puts her hands on the ground in front of her, her feet apart. Spectators respond immediately with approving sounds, almost saying 'yeah!' She is confused, but looks happy. She lets her body down onto the floor by letting her feet slide backwards. Spectators groan. She is more confused, and laughing more, as are we. She wonders what this could be. She lifts one hand and rolls cautiously onto her back and keeps rolling as we laugh. Then several quick rolls. She suddenly feels like she knows and goes onto all fours and crawls towards the centre again. Spectators groan and she stops and returns to where she just was. Then tries sudden movements as if to stand, like a frog leaping. We laugh at how wrong it is. How could she think this was right? She doesn't understand why we are laughing. She laughs uncontrollably. She tries the jump again. No reaction. She crawls a little, then back, her eyes on us always, testing our reactions. Both hands are on the floor, one knee also, the other leg is straight with the foot on the floor. Tentatively, without knowing what to do, she raises the knee from the floor and we laugh make approving noises as her legs straighten. It's clear now to her and she bends her elbows to do a single press-up, then collapses in laughter as we scream with delight and applaud. The exercise has lasted just over four minutes.

From this single example, we can deduce that laughter and approval work differently. Our pleasure, expressed through laughter, often occurs when the performer is lost, but not when she is not checking in with us. Just being lost is not, in itself, agreeable to us. Likewise, getting close to doing what we decided would be the show does not, in itself, delight us.

The exercise leads us to examine our feelings about ignorance in front of others (if we are the performer) and our feelings about knowing more than others (if we are the spectators). To squeeze the most out of this exercise in terms of exploration of feelings, it's good to let the performer sink or swim, with no conscious 'help'.

CASE STUDY 14.2

BA Theatre and Performance Practice, London Metropolitan University, November 2019

With this group, we pushed further out beyond the exercise as such. The task became:

- Plan a trio/duo scene, then perform it but only if audience is 'engaged'.
- This can be understood as a wider scope of reactions than laughter.
- As in 'Guess the Show' you have learned to identify a range of audience reactions:
  - Laughter
  - Silence
  - Excitement, sitting forward
  - Boredom, slumping
  - Clenched fists
  - Barely controlled shrieks of excitement
  - Eyes unfocused
  - Eyes focused on something particular, a part of the space, a part of your body, etc.

These are some of the 'clues' that led you towards what the audience had in mind.

Now, the audience has nothing in mind, but you must elicit these responses if you are to continue with your planned performance. So you will perform only when they laugh, are shocked, lean forward, shriek, or whatever.

One performer might manage this audience engagement, whilst the others are involved only in their fictional world.

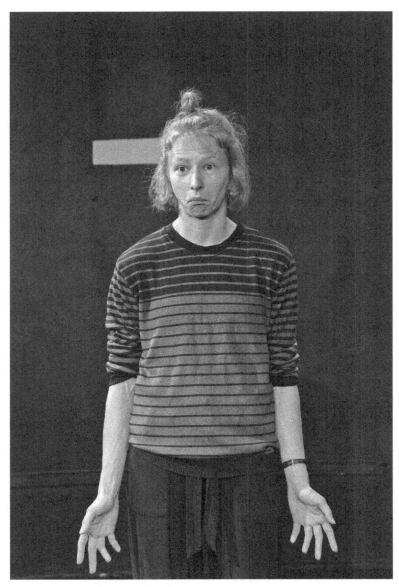

Figure 9 I Feel Stupid: Giedre Degutyte.

15
FEELING SHIT

The previous few exercises here have all placed the participants before an audience in order to see what feelings arise and how we can play them. Getting up in front of others is always going to elicit plenty of feelings, but, hopefully, the stakes are not too high such that the situation might cause the performers to shut down. Exactly how to judge this is up to the teacher and group in the moment. The point is for everyone to explore, not to dismantle the performers in some misguided belief that they need to be broken down, stripped bare, or otherwise reduced to a mythical neutral state. Let the individual performers control how far they want to go, in tandem with gentle coaxing from the teacher. In many ways, this is a parallel skill to working with audiences. How far do they want to go? Let them decide. Chucking stuff at an audience or pushing them into participation without their consent, for example, is pointless and at best the mark of a clumsy performance.

There has always been a certain controversy in some circles surrounding some approaches to clown teaching which emphasize putting the student 'in the shit'. Often lumped together under the title of 'via negativa' the criticism usually centres on a perception that this pedagogy involves abusive behaviour on the part of the teacher. Its defenders often point to the teachers' intentions being kindly, via a method which is only playfully hierarchical (e.g. in the case of Gaulier), though this defence probably doesn't hold water for all individual clown teachers who follow this route. Particularly in our current times, when in the West we are questioning privilege and marginalization, the fact that clowning is ostensibly practised, taught and learned by white people in Europe and North America is beginning to be challenged and one of the potential culprits is the emphasis on putting students in states of vulnerability, which favours the socially non-vulnerable (the white, the male, the straight, the abled) and disadvantages those who in their

174 THE CLOWNING WORKBOOK

day-to-day life are vulnerable due to their identity. This is a hugely important shift in thinking, but we are just at the beginning of it.

CASE STUDY 15.1

Comedy Module, BA Drama, Liverpool John Moores University, October 2017

Consent, consent, consent

Sometimes, a group happens that urges us towards looking at things from a specific viewpoint which other groups wouldn't want to touch. In this case, a group of students who had opted to study comedy in its many facets, became excited by the idea that clowning looked like a kind of consensual bullying, as we came to describe it.

While doing the exercise of do what you want then check if we laugh and if not get punished, in a circle, one student began to be the butt of the jokes. As it was funny once when someone took his glasses, others tried the same tactic to see if it was still funny, following the principle of repetition in clowning. It was funny. He became more and more the victim.

In discussions afterwards, there was general agreement that everyone knew that this 'victim' was volunteering to be the butt.

16
PERSONAL CLOWN SKILLS

This section looks at some ways to devise new clown exercises and teaching in a way that is personal yet does not demand that the student be 'vulnerable', or 'in the shit'.

So far, we've explored feeling through the prism of what we experience when performing in front of others. But that experience, depending on how it is framed, can be a damaging, rather than a learning experience. If the teaching method assumes that, before a student can learn something, they have to be brought to some kind of state of *tabula rasa* (philosophically, the 'blank slate' which supposedly precedes the imprinting of ideas and knowledge upon us)[1] – then this already excludes the knowledge that the student comes to the training with. That knowledge may be extremely rich, culturally specific or highly determined by their identity, experience or social context. It may be that, paradoxically, trying to start from 'nothing' ends up producing pretty much the same result in each person, rather than drawing on each one's actual lived experience.

How can we tap into this knowledge? And can we learn it from each other? The following scopes out some initial ways forward in what is, to my knowledge, an entirely new approach to clown teaching.[2]

16.1 Self-reflection

Each person takes some time to reflect and make notes for themselves, addressing the question:

- Which aspects of your social identity do you feel place you out of the norm, either mostly, sometimes or occasionally? (This can

176   THE CLOWNING WORKBOOK

be anything from gender, ethnicity, disability to mental health, neuro-divergency, body type, or family habits, personal eccentricities.)

The thinking behind this is a common assumption we have that clowns are a kind of staging of the marginal, or excluded.[3] Is this true? Let's assume it is and see where it takes us. Does it let us ask interesting new questions? Find interesting new exercises? Spark interest in new students?

The reflective process started here allows for a more considered approach to exploring your own personal experience than usually happens when you are thrown onto a stage only to be ejected immediately because you're 'not funny'.

16.2 Sharing your reflections

In pairs or small groups, share whichever reflections you wish. Ask each other questions like:

- In what situations does this manifest?
- How do you react?
- How does it determine your behaviour?
- What do you feel?

16.3 Teaching your knowledge

- Share with the whole group.
- Can the shared knowledge be 'staged'?
- Can the shared knowledge be 'taught'?

By 'knowledge' here is meant the specific and repeatable ways in which one person behaves and responds to experiencing marginalization or being regarded as not fitting in with expectations, society's norms. Can that behaviour be demonstrated and can others copy it (learn it)?

Here are some examples:

CASE STUDY 16.1

Research workshop, Clown Symposium 'State of Play', Edge Hill University, December 2018

OC shared that being much shorter than most people he knew made him feel different. Together we explored what that meant in practice.

OC stands next to me. Our heights are grossly out of balance. People laugh. OC is happy to expose himself in this way and full consent to be laughed at is given. He is experienced and comfortable being laughed at.

I ask if we could use this knowledge to teach students of clowning who do not have this experience. I ask him if there is anything he habitually DOES in response to his shortness. 'Doing' is the basis of both performance and of performer training. He says he tends to look down at the floor, to avoid gazing upwards constantly. He demonstrates. Laughs from the audience.

I ask if he would mind trying one of my exercises, the Step-Laugh. He is happy to do so and walks across the stage from wing to wing, taking a step every time we laugh. I then ask him to do the exercise again, but to look down at the floor. This time he is funnier. Then again, and I ask him to consciously make use of the looking down action to save himself from no laughs. Success. It is clear that, at least for him, this action 'works' and produces clowning. It could well be that this success is dependent on his height alone. I ask others to try the exercise and use the downward looking. It seems like it does transfer to others, but not necessarily to everyone, nor in all instances. However, it IS a new option to be added to potential exercises.

In this new exercise, then, there is no vulnerability, no shit, no failure.

Another example:

LA and AR have been talking about how being mothers of young babies made them feel marginalized, that their behaviour had become 'other' for the rest of society. This was felt to be experienced when they refused to accept advice from others, feeling that they, as mother, instinctively knew what was best for their child. This can overflow into other contexts, leading to an overly bossy stance. We tried to re-enact this onstage but it dragged into a wordy dialogue trying to explain an idea, rather than a series of actions that could be done and repeated. One aspect that came up was that the mother would feel disengaged from, or uncommitted to, maintaining the conversation, prioritizing her own needs as being those of her baby. For example, by turning away from a conversation. We staged this. And then simply walking away in the middle of a dialogue. This was extremely funny and easily repeatable, by other people, too.

This exercise proved later to be popular, especially with students who have difficulty working out how they feel, or in a diverse group that enjoys sharing their differences and reflections on their own personal-life-clown-skills which they already possessed.

16.4 Clowning socially

This approach can also lead a group to consider how much they already know. And not just via the 'negatives' which this section has been exploring. Once you realize how much you do know, you may realize how much you already clown in your life.

Ask yourself:

- Do I already clown in my day-to-day life?
- In which contexts do I clown socially?
- In my family?
- With my partner?
- Playing sport?
- At work?
- Going clubbing all night?
- During religious events?

Can you teach some of these to others?

PART THREE

'THAT WAS SUPPOSED TO BE FUNNY'

During our explorations so far, we've worked on conditioning that aids in attending to audience's responses and performers' responses. We've paid attention to what is happening in the moment of performing (or doing an exercise designed to replicate one aspect of performing). In many of these exercises, we've followed a regular sequence both spatially:

- Begin in a circle.
- Then end-on, with performers and spectators facing each other.

And in content:

- First with 'scripted' game actions (throw the ball, catch the ball, tag someone, etc.).
- Then with free-form improvised actions.

In some cases we've also added the option of deciding what you're going to do before beginning. In Part Three we will look in more detail how to use 'pre-decided scripts', or 'plans'.

180 THE CLOWNING WORKBOOK

Contemporary clown training has tended to ignore scripting, preferring to concentrate on what happens 'in the moment'. This is not surprising, given that clown workshops emerged historically in a period (late 1950s–early 1960s) when the 'text' was deemed 'tyrannous' and the planned or scripted was mistrusted as just another way to restrict personal expression. This search for spontaneity found its application across all artforms, not just clowning, from dance to ceramics, jazz to poetry, painting to psychotherapy and philosophy.[1] To put it simply, 'everyone was thinking the same way'. In clowning, the previous generations came quickly to be regarded as irrelevant.[2]

I have previously written in detail about the usefulness of drawing on that older tradition, the clowning that has a repertoire of scenes, gags, props, styles, and re-applying it now in order to create clown performance material which works for us now. Here, however, I will not be looking at devising methods as such, but instead how we can train ourselves by using plans and scripts as one facet of what performance entails. The play between script and performance (with all that entails in clown–audience interaction, and state of mind, feeling and body whilst clowning) is a rich source for clowns, and to deny ourselves one side of that game is to have a much poorer game indeed.

So: what do clowns do with scripts? What plans do they have? What do clowns do with others' scripts? And what do we end up with as a result?

17
FUNNY PLANS

Using scripts can seem like quite advanced clowning. In one sense, that is so. But it can also be a marvellous starting point for any training. We've already incorporated planned actions of varying complexity in many of the exercises. This section goes a step further and explores plans with the intention of being funny.

I've grown to prefer the term 'plan' to 'script', as plans can be in any format: written down at length, in a few notes, or in our heads. Scripts are assumed to be written down and are often associated with a single writer. It is useful, however, to recycle the term 'script' for our own context of clowning, in order to take some of the heat out of the idea that clowns 'just make it up'. And there's no reason why clowns can't have written scripts.[1]

17.1 Make a funny plan

- In pairs or small groups, agree on a funny plan together, that you will then perform for everyone else.
- To be a plan, it must be fundamentally decided what you are going to do: who, when, how, and so on. No improvisation.
- To be a funny plan, the intention of your plan must be to make others laugh.

17.1.1 Perform the funny plan

- Perform what you agreed as planned.
- Make it clear when you have finished (take a bow) and see what effect it has.

What does the audience think?

- Is it clear when you wanted us to laugh?
- Is it clear why you wanted us to laugh?

These are the questions which this exercise is designed to test. **Not** whether we actually laughed or not. In other words, were the performers' **intentions** clear?

17.1.2 Re-perform the funny plan

There are a number of useful ways to re-perform your plan. If the intention to be funny is clear, then:

- Perform only the funny bits (the bits you intended to be funny, whether people laughed or not).
- Move as quickly as possible to the next 'laughter point' (the point where you **expect** people to laugh).

Or:

- Don't continue to the next laughter point until you have got a laugh from the previous one.
- Use any means at your disposal (planned or otherwise) to get the laugh. Then move on in your plan.

If, on the other hand, your original plan proved not to be clear in its intentions to make us laugh, add the following:

- At each moment you intended us to laugh, say 'That was supposed to be funny'.
- If we then laugh, continue with your plan.
- If we still don't laugh, add: 'That was supposed to be funny, because . . .' and then explain why you thought it was going to be funny.
- Keep explaining until we laugh. Then continue with your plan.

FUNNY PLANS

Or even:

- Explain what is happening all of the time so that you make sure we understand, even the bits which are not supposed to be funny. (If you find yourself doing a lot of mimed or fictional actions that we didn't 'get', this can be great fun.)

These options can also usefully be employed on a funny plan which was clear originally.

The act of telling us that you thought that we were going to laugh is often a good provocation for us to laugh. Not only was your idea not funny, but you really did think it was going to be funny – how ridiculous of you! Even more ridiculous, if you then have to explain why we were supposed to laugh.[2]

The intention to be funny

Planning ahead, intending to be funny, brings with it a whole new scale of stage emotions. Now, not only will you be in front of an audience, but there will be expectations. I would guess that for many people, if public speaking is a fear, then having to be funny is a greater fear.

The expectation of laughter defines the genre of clowning. That doesn't mean that everything will be 'trying to be funny'. The basic intention gives rise to a complex and unexpected art form which is clowning.

Sometimes, we want to laugh but don't. Because we know the intention is to make us laugh, we come to a show either ready to laugh or ready to not laugh. Or even to resist laughing. Laughter isn't just spontaneous. Not only is it set up, or expected by means of the genre rules (comedy), but it is also adjusted by the audience's will. To laugh or not to laugh.

But although this will feel like a big risk, the failure to be funny will quickly become a great, if not a greater, pleasure, than being funny. Herein lies the true flop. The greater the intention, the greater the fall, and the greater the laugh and the pleasure for all.

Don't be in a hurry. This flop may only come at the very end of your plan, when you bow. As well as bowing, try saying 'thank you' or 'sorry'. Saying sorry is a great way to establish a correct relationship between you the clown and us the audience. You are always at fault, always the guilty party.

If you are enjoying this exercise and want to increase the feeling you get from the risk:

- announce the plan before you start, and
- promise it will be funny.

17.2 On-script and off-script

It might be that you get audience reaction from

- your original script;
- the way you modify how you perform your original script (intensifying it, slowing it down, etc.);
- doing something else that wasn't in the script.

Using off-script actions in order to get reactions that then allow you to continue with your plan is an entirely legitimate and useful strategy. Make sure you distinguish clearly between:

- on-script actions: they are planned beforehand;
- off-script actions: they are improvised.

This exercise 'solves' the age-old 'problem' of the relationship between script and improvisation. They both have their place, and play off each other. The script gives you an obligation to do something, which obliges you to be judged (flop), so the script is an aid to flopping. In short, scripts produce clowning!

You can think that the off-script choices are there to help you feel funny, or to help your partner(s) feel funny if it is their turn to advance the plan and they are stuck.

It may be that these off-scripts will take up more space than your script. Which is fine. It may look to the audience that this is your 'clown persona'.

Or you may be the kind of clown that is always on-script, if your plan turns out to be funny without help.

FUNNY PLANS 185

If you find that some of your off-script choices are really effective, then you can incorporate them into a revised plan. Likewise with any modifications to how you deliver your plan. This now becomes a live devising process which uses your audience to fine-tune your performance. The act of creating and performing becomes the performance.

17.3 Plans with feelings

- Make plans.
- When performing the plan, say after each action what you feel (three options of funny/not funny/stupid).
- If you get a feeling in the midst of doing a planned action, say it!

17.3.1 Plans leading to more feelings and more actions

- Same as before, but if you feel funny or stupid **after** your planned action is done, then do something else, unplanned/ off-script, **as long as that feeling stupid/funny lasts**. Actually, this off-script action can be an elaboration of your scripted action.
- Then, once the stupid/funny feeling has subsided, go back to your scripted plan.

17.3.2 Plans only when you feel

- Now, only perform your plan when you feel funny/stupid.
- If you don't feel it, don't do it.
- When you don't feel funny, you are free to do any off-script actions, until your funny/stupid feeling kicks in and you go back on-script.

In other words:

- Make funny plans that you THINK will be so funny.
- Perform your plan, but only continue when you FEEL it (or you) is going to be funny.
- In pairs or trios: when you don't feel stupid, then you don't perform, but your partner might do. Then you feel stupid! The rhythm of your feeling stupid will be your performance rhythm.

This combines the best of both worlds: structured composition together with in-the-moment performance.

17.4 Types of plan

It would be tedious and ineffective to try to explain all the dos and don'ts of plans before trying this exercise. Far better to make all kinds of plans and then reflect on which ones are best for your clowning. Here are some common outcomes:

- **Linear, consequential plans**. We see how 'one thing leads to another'. Often seen in classically structured jokes. For example. Person X walks across stage, Person Y trips them up.[3] (Away from the genre of clowning, the so-called 'well-made play' also follows this format.)[4] It's easy to follow as it's obvious. That's an advantage in this exercise. As it's obvious, it's difficult for such a gag to be funny (surprise is lacking), so that's also good for this exercise, and you will have to work to find a way to make us laugh!
- **Non-linear plans**. These seem 'abstract' and often depend for their humour more on execution than content. This might include the personality of the performer, or the timing, for example. This kind of plan is tricky to use in this exercise, as it is already relying on the performance (the second part of the exercise). So there is little contrast between script and performance. And it's that contrast which is your friend.

FUNNY PLANS

- **Performance scripts** (songs, dances, etc.). These are very easy for an audience to go along with without question and are therefore easy to work with in this exercise. We are not wondering 'what is this?' and are therefore content to watch how the clown performs, not what they perform.

- **Fictional worlds.** Trying to create times and places which are not the here and now is hard work. Both for performer and audience. It doesn't leave much room for us to watch 'how' you are performing for us, as it funnels our attention into 'what'. Extreme cases would be illusionistic mime, or complex whodunnits.

- **Tasks in the theatre** (or circus, or street, or hospital or wherever you are performing)**.** In stark contrast to fictional worlds, these are actions which the audience will not question, because they belong and are expected in the place in which we find ourselves. Examples might be:

  - Jobs in the theatre: clean the stage, operate lights, stage management.
  - Circus: set up equipment, clean up.
  - Street: cross the street, stop the traffic, ask for directions.

- **Games.** Occasionally, when asked to come up with a plan, people might use a set of rules. In a certain way, this could be called a plan. But the outcomes are always uncertain, so there will be little contrast between plan and performance. Keep the plan predictable, and let the performance be uncertain.[5]

Whether you prefer to call them linear, or coherent, or obvious, it's those kinds of plans which leave room for us to clown while the action takes care of itself.

CASE STUDY 17.1

Devising class, London Clown School, May 2019

HM has brought some ideas for a clown number. She has a bag with a cloth, glasses, candle, wine carton, phone. We work on clarifying her script, thinking of it as a plan to amuse us, rather than a 'scene' or 'situation' that she must create.

Jon: What is the joke? Imagine it was a verbal joke: set up and punchline. This would be a basic funny plan structure. For example, you have a date, it's on Tinder, you have a date with the photo and then leave the photo. Then repeat, x 3, so it's a 'Rule of 3' structure.

If it's simply a funny plan format, then all the set-ups need to be as concise as possible, otherwise there's lots of stuff that isn't funny, nor serving our amusement.

The set-ups can be as long as that, but they would also need structuring to be funny in themselves, into 3s, or something 'wrong'. What's a funny way to pour out the drink? What's the silly rhythm of those objects in normal use?

This way, the whole number is full of 'That was supposed to be funny'.

Or: play the scene as is, but only advancing with laughs each step. This forces you to find something funny, most probably off-script. It might be a silly gag, a face, a trousers drop, or an intensely stupid voice or way of moving.

Plus: get a distance from the emotions. Emotions can be hilarious, but only when you find what's ridiculous about them: are they expressed in a silly way? Are they expressed in the wrong moment? The 'right' emotion in the 'right' way won't amuse us.

Ideally, you would use both approaches, Step-Laugh and Funny Plan.

FUNNY PLANS   189

CASE STUDY 17.2

Public open workshop, Victoria & Albert Museum 'Friday Late', April 2018

Grasping the notion of what a plan is, is key to making this exercise work for you. Funny plans can be encapsulated in a task which includes both the action and the intention. This does not necessarily require hours and hours of studio or class time, but is a concept anyone can understand.

In this public workshop, the concept was introduced 'on the go' and participants encouraged to try the following out on other visitors to the museum.

Prop-based funny plans

A box of modified objects was supplied. Each object was designed with a particular humorous effect built in, for example:[6]

- a pack of cards stapled together so that they never fall but can be 'shuffled';
- a slapstick;
- a squirting camera;
- a whoopee cushion.

Each person is then invited to:

- choose a clown prop;
- familiarize yourself with the 'joke';
- find someone passing by and get eye contact;
- time the delivery to try and elicit a laugh.

17.5 Funny plans and simple scripts

If we cast ourselves back to using simple scripts (not obligatorily funny ones) in the exercise Step-Laugh, we can say that there were a few broad categories:

190　THE CLOWNING WORKBOOK

- The script isn't funny in itself, so you play off-script things in order to advance.
- The script isn't funny, but you find a funny way to play it.
- The script is funny in itself (things in the script make us laugh).
- We find you funny for any unknown reason.

This is worth remembering if your 'supposed to be funny' plans fall flat. You have many other options for responding to absence of laughter:

- Let us know your feelings about your performance.
- Express how you feel about your co-performers – communicate with other clowns (arguing about what's next, prompting).
- Or about the audience.
- State the obvious.
- Commentate on what's there, on what is happening.

Ideally the laughter will end up matching your performance energy. It IS your performance energy.

How do you clown when your story, your characters aren't funny? How to find funny ways of doing or saying things, off-script things?

When the actor goes back a step because their dramatic emotion expression hasn't landed well in the audience, and then we laugh, they are reenergized with pleasure and advance emoting with new force, a force which 'convinces' us, makes us laugh.

The Step-Laugh script basically ties the actor to the audience in the here and now of the live performance. Once you've learned to do this with the easy response of laughter (which is objective and indisputable), then you can do it with other, less obvious responses. This way you have fun playing a role, such that we will say 'yes, go on!'

Try this also:

- Enter the stage using Step-Laugh.
- On reaching centre stage, do your funny plan, regardless of audience reaction.
- Exit the stage using Step-Laugh.

FUNNY PLANS

- Or: 'Reverse Step-Laugh' (you must stay if it's funny). If during your exit, there are laughs, you must return and re-do your plan (even if the plan is awfully unfunny).

This is particularly silly if your performance of your plan has been an awful disaster, as you are now obliged to relive your nightmare! Such fun!

Conclusions: Funny plans and the 'clown's situation'

Hopefully now it is clearer how scripts and plans, especially ones that are supposed to be funny, are your friend. In fact, all of this section reproduces what we could call the 'clown's situation' itself.

The clown's situation is:

- You've made a funny plan.
- You're here in front of an audience doing the funny plan.
- You don't know when people will laugh.
- How do you respond?

The next situation then occurs:

- You've performed your funny plan.
- You can predict it's 20% funny, for example.
- You have to repeat it.
- How do you respond?

Your responses can be:

- Oh shit! (flop).
- OK, I'll do this (fart, dance, whatever) to make them laugh at this intended laughter point.
- I'll do it differently, more intensely, less intensely, any way until they like it.
- Explain WHY it's supposed to be funny.

Figure 10 That Was Supposed to Be Funny: Kaisa Koskinen, Camille Suarez.

18
INTRUDERS

There are plenty of theories around that perceive clowns as imposters, intruders, accidental or unwanted presences which disrupt an otherwise orderly, conventional or predictable context, whether the latter be a theatre play, a circus act or the traffic. Or indeed any self-defined serious context from politics to the sacred. There are also notions of clowns being the centre of attention, the crowd-pleasing master of ceremonies, with other events being peripheral.

My own first formal experience of clowning was as what looks like an intruder, the character of Bobby Trot who enters the stage in an early Victorian melodrama looking for his bundle while everyone else is dealing with traumatic events designed to elicit spectators' responses of anger and tears. And there are many examples of popular performance genres throughout history and across cultures which find no problems mixing the earnest meaningfulness of narratives with the apparent pointlessness of clowns which seem to continually be dissolving that meaning.[1]

This section explores exercises to understand and practise some of the dynamics of that relationship between orderly meaning and disruptive clowning. This mostly entails using a (serious) plan, together with a separate comic intention, so we will be building on a number of the concepts already dealt with in this book.

18.1 Intrude on an organized performance

- Divide up into small groups or pairs and devise a short performance in any style (it's easier if the style is not comic).

- Make out that you know what you are doing (as with previous work with plans and scripts).
- Perform each piece as it is for everyone else to see (with no expectations of laughter).

Now we will add the intruder, or clown, element:

- Perform each piece again, but now have one extra person, from outside the group, join you.
- The intruder can join the performance at any point – at first, it may be wise to wait a little and work out how you are going to intrude.

What is the role of the intruder? Rather than trying to understand this in an abstract way, we can give the intruder an objective task:

- The intruder is responsible for making the audience laugh.
- The actors will only continue when there is laughter.

Or:

- The actors can only continue when there is NO laughter.

What can the intruder do? Anything that elicits laughter. Once you have done this exercise a few times, you will start to see patterns, or options emerging. Some common ones for the intruder are:

- Join in and try to be part of their show.
- Destroy or spoil their show.
- Comment or commentate on their show.
- Walk through their show.
- Be near them, without proposing anything of your own.
- Laugh.
- Do your own show.
- Help the actors.
- Physically restrain the actors.

INTRUDERS

- Block our view, or the actors' view between themselves.
- Steal props.
- Bring new objects.
- Bring new costumes.
- Switch the lights on and off.
- Play music.
- Ask questions.
- Look at the audience.
- Make asides to the audience.
- Annoy people in general however you can.

The main point to grasp here is your task, which is to elicit laughter by means of intruding on a performance you do not form part of. You may have heard of ways of characterizing a clown's behaviour, such as 'clowns always do their best' or 'clowns are interested in things'. These characterizations may be true for some clowns some of the time, but they do not describe your intentions as a performer, so they can never be the basis upon which you build your clowning. They are interpretations after the event, at best, and as such do not serve the clown performer.

But this exercise is not just about the intruder. The actors must respond in some way or another. So, what are the actors' options or strategies?

- Incorporate the clowns – find a way to include the clown's behaviour in order to maintain the integrity of the performance.
- Ignore the clowns – carry on as if they weren't there.
- Reply to the clowns – to try and divert their intrusion, or to stop it.
- Restrain the clowns – physically remove the clown from the stage, for example.

In all these cases, the actors' task is to maintain the integrity of their performance.[2]

18.1.1 Intrude on an existing performance

Some groups already have some bits of non-clown performance available to show (drama students will typically be working on a number of different pieces at the same time with their classmates). If this is your case:

- Divide up into small groups or pairs who can together present a short performance that they have already rehearsed elsewhere.
- Or make sure at least one person in each group has a piece they can quickly teach the others.
- Perform each piece as it is for everyone else to see.

The more detailed and accurate you can be, the better, whether it's words or actions.

Then, as before, we introduce an intruding performer.

18.1.2 Pair of intruders

Now introduce two clown intruders at the same time. There are several broad strategies open to the pair of clowns:

- Discuss your strategy and work together.
- Go solo.
- Take turns.
- Work against each other.

18.2 Reverse intrusion

Once the above is clear, try doing the intrusion in reverse:

- One or more performers devise a funny plan together.
- They begin their funny plan performance.
- Another performer, who has not been part of their plan, intrudes.

- This performer can only do things designed NOT to make us laugh.

The original clown performer(s) then have similar options to the serious actors described earlier, in that the clowns can incorporate, ignore, reply to, or restrain the serious intruder(s). This may in some way approximate to the idea mentioned earlier, that clowns control the stage whilst serious actors are trapped, bullied, ridiculed or otherwise exploited.

18.3 Classical clowning

There are other ways to conceive of these dynamics. In 'classical circus clowning' (the so-called Golden Age roughly between 1870 and 1939)[3] it is often the case that the 'whiteface clown' (originally referred to simply as 'Clown') will have a stated aim or objective to achieve, such as a magic trick, playing a piece of music, displaying acrobatic prowess, or playing a prank on someone else. The 'Auguste' (the type of clown which in the last half century has been the model for most clown training) will then typically interrupt, disrupt, intrude, annoy or otherwise delay and hinder the achievement of the former's desire. This hindrance will often be seemingly motivated by such 'innocent' drives as hunger or thirst, wanting to help, or the desire to be included.

We can easily recycle the dynamics of this clown drama by using the principles in an exercise:

- One person decides on a clear aim (something which they can actually achieve here and now).
- They begin to perform this for us.
- A second person enters having chosen a motivating drive such as to help, to accompany, to be included or whatever.

The aims can be simple and non-comic, as in the non-funny plans, as simple as 'tidying the chairs'. The more material and do-able, the better.

18.4 Multiple intrusions

Classical circus clowning has many examples of acts based on sequences of intrusions. The following format and exercise were devised by extracting the dramaturgical principles of the one well-known example.[4]

Here is the sequence:

1 Whiteface clown (WF) enters and makes their intentions clear (to achieve something).
2 First Auguste (A1) enters and does something intrusive, disruptive, or in any way 'wrong'.
3 A1 exits and WF continues with their plan.
4 Second Auguste (A2) enters and does something intrusive, disruptive, or in any way 'wrong'.
5 A2 exits and WF continues with their plan.
6 A1 enters, with a new interruption, exits, and WF continues.
7 A2 enters, with a new interruption, exits, and WF continues.
8 A1 and A2 enter together.
9 WF, A1 and A2 all do something together successfully (with NO problems).
10 All exit.

This can be extended or shortened as you will.

- You can have a single Auguste, or several.
- They can interrupt multiple times or just once.
- The Augustes can even interrupt each other.[5]

The interruptions can either:

- relate to the WF's main objective (for example, if the WF is intending to play music, the Auguste's actions might also be musical);

INTRUDERS

or

- NOT relate to the WF's main objective (for example, relating more to the venue, the stage, the audience, or the Auguste's own obsession).

The successful action at the end can either:

- relate to the WF's aim;

or

- be something completely unconnected (just a dance or a song to finish on).

This success might look unexpected to you here. Feel free to omit it if you prefer. But first do try and see what curious effect it can have. After all this coming and going and delayed gratification, the success not only leaves us on an 'up', but it can also serve as a kind of admission that all this clowning was not 'real' at all, but just a joke. In a way, it is a joke distancing of the clowning itself. It is saying, well, you thought these people were stupid clowns, but actually we're just having you on. It's a celebration which breaks the form. And clowns love to break forms. We've been fooled. Personally, I like the notion that clowns are not 'really' clowns, as it upends the sometimes overly earnest insistence on 'authenticity', which seems so un-clown-like to my taste.

As with the previous exercises in this section, if you are playing the WF role you have a number of options on how to respond (ignore, incorporate, restrain). Whiteface clowns do not have fixed characters, the role can be benign, disdainful, authoritarian, helpful, nurturing or violent.[6]

CASE STUDY 18.1

BA European Theatre Arts students and graduates, Rose Bruford College, London, September 2017

A new path to the same place presented itself one day. We were playing a children's game called 'Barley Break', just to focus on something non-performative for a short time. The game involves pairs of players holding hands and having to find new partners, and whoever ends up without a partner can be tagged by the person who is on it.[7]

How do I have fun?

Keeping people out for a long time?

Being alone?

Switching around?

It was apparent that players' pleasure can emerge from any of the outcomes in this game: pairing up, being left alone, catching someone, being happy to remain outside, spoiling others' plans. Several players observed how much they enjoyed being the outsider, which allowed for a greater contact with the audience than if you were locked into maintaining your couple.

Jon When you're on your own, you're a clown . . . the outsider . . .

LH Then you include the audience, who were also feeling like an outsider.

Jon Exactly. If we take the third person out, what do we have?

PW A fourth wall.

Jon When you have the outsider, you have the clown in what would otherwise be a fourth wall situation. It's fun and funny to be pair-less, the outsider. Can I disrupt or spoil their interaction? There is another clown definition: someone who spoils others' things.

- One pair sings a duet. The intruder uses blatantly pretended emotions in an attempt to gain our attention. Their acting style is lying, deceitful, a

INTRUDERS

201

set of mercenary emotions to get what they want. Could this be the essence of all acting? The fake emotions clearly arise as a means to their objective, which is to disrupt by drawing attention. The use of acting to obtain a non-fictional (there is no 'as if' required), real stage task (attention/disruption) is fascinating.

Jon When you play an emotion, what's the difference between being the actor in the piece and the clown outsider? The clown expression comes from a different place: a desperate need to please? In order to achieve something else. I'm playing this emotion so that I can get the audience attention. It has a mercenary function. But what's different to other methods of acting? If you just took that bit of acting, and asked 'how do you do that?'

LH It's more truthful.

Jon But no, look at LS's acting, it was fake.

LH Truthful in the sense that it chimes with us the audience.

Jon If it's played, we know you're lying, then that is the acting method: lying. If LS had really felt that need [to express the emotion] then it might feel too personal, painful. But then all acting is pretence, lying.

HE Is it because you reveal something about the clown?

Jon But LS doesn't 'want' that attention as a person. She wants it because her assigned role is the clown/outsider.

- HD and NP perform an abstract visual duo, using symbolic hand gestures to represent church, heart, circle. LH, the intruder, does not attempt to inhabit their created 'other' time/space, so we now have two worlds co-existing. LH takes the symbols literally as if they were actually these places and objects and 'enters' the church, for example. This is a kind of taking 'fiction literally'. HD and NP continue on their more abstract plane, maintaining a rhythm of change of shapes, not suggesting a siting or content. LH takes a new tactic, placing herself in the physical midst, and looks through their picture at the audience, like a window. We laugh.

One might have assumed it difficult for clowns to engage with abstract theatre, but of course, being abstract, it is the kind of theatre most fictionally distant from the reality of the theatre space, and hence an easy 'target' for clowns who live in the here and now. The shapes made by the actors were constant, good for a clown disruption. The intruder knew what was coming up next so she can be one step ahead, whilst they are locked into a script. The original survives, at the same time as being disrupted.

Jon The time thing is going on, while you are in a different time. You two are creating the space-time thing, while LH is in another dimension. In the same space and time, but not in this other world, just in this world. It's a bit like being invisible, like those stories of ghosts, 'why can't they see me?'

Acting styles? LH's presence is with us. She tries to bring it back down to earth, although it also used more complex forms of performance, more character/situation.

- LS and HE perform a naturalistic situation: hair styling. How can PW the clown intruder successfully get into their game? And how to react?

Jon The intruder here needs to find the focal point and intrude just there [to LS and HE]. Try responding to PW, one or both of you.

HE I didn't know how to stop her without ruining my game.

Jon Ah! It might ruin your game. If you say, No I can't, go away! Give her instructions. How do we get people to do what we want them to do? By verbal command, physical force or restraint.

As intruder, you got into the space where they were. Another tactic, you don't have to get into their situation, you can create a whole new thing, put music on, put lights on, throw a bucket of water on them, do a dance. One way is to try and get in. Or you can just stand here and sigh. Or cry in the corner.

- OH and LH perform a 'wheelbarrow pair' with one holding the legs of the other who has their hands on the floor. HE intrudes by tickling LH's feet, then HE sits on LH, and takes her feet, then takes OH's feet. They swap. HE tries to piggyback. LH invites HE to be the wheelbarrow.

INTRUDERS

203

OH is offended. HE won't let her legs be lifted. OH has become the outsider.

The original two performers have difficulty maintaining it when the intruder physically interferes, and argue about what their plan is. In their attempt to maintain order, they become ridiculous clowns themselves, breaking their own order. One of them offered the intruder a role, and this backfired. This is fun. Although the places in the trio switched, OH always tried to maintain the original order and HE always had the drive to spoil. With clowns, simple drives or motivations produce much: maintain, create, disrupt, destroy.

The exercise proves very popular with these acting students. It seems to embody so many of the demands they encounter, but in a way that allows them to be bad actors, attention-seeking actors, actors who deliberately spoil others' acting. We chat about how this exercise could be a fun staging of the dynamics of groups in reality:

Jon   It's so similar to class – you're trying to devise a great piece of performance, and one person in your group says 'oh but we could do this'. 'No, we rehearsed it', 'oh but I could be this'. 'I'll just improvise!'

We all laugh because it's so familiar to all of us. Can this liberate us a little from the pressure to come up with coherent, creative or 'good' ideas?

Jon   In clowning, you accept an expectation, and break it.

HD   Always?

Jon   It's a good rule. At some point you will. Like jokes – punchlines break the expectation, the setup. You might wait a whole hour before breaking it. Or it might happen on entry. The impulse to contradict – it's fun and a good thing to cultivate. As soon as you recognize something, chuck it in the bin.

HD   What if it's working, though?

Jon   Well, it's not about whether it works or not. it's about seeing it as a thing. Identify the thing first, only then can you spoil it. If you can't recognize

204 THE CLOWNING WORKBOOK

it, you can't break it. At any moment there is a context being created. It's not an individual thing. Find the context and act against it.

They devise new performances to be intruded upon.

- SP and NP measure space with spans of arms. LS intrudes. SP asks, 'Do you want to help? Stand there and do this. Yes, good . . . No . . . Good, yeah . . .' LS trips NP and apologizes then shouts 'No that's wrong!' then shouts out numbers. LS: 'I don't know what to do!' NP: 'We can do the floor instead.' LS has laid down on floor already.

Jon It was good that the pair tried to adapt. Yes, adapting is fine. One thing I'm not sure about, is that politeness in clowning. When you say, could you please. My instinct would be to be more direct.

LS I found it quite funny, the politeness.

Jon Yes, maybe because you were so rude!

Jon Really try to actually really disrupt it, rather than making a show. We said before that the clown's emotion was pretend, but the intention was actually to disrupt. So the acting is pretence, lie, fake, but the real task is to disrupt. By using, mercenarily, the pretend acting. It may be akin to Stanislavski's idea of the task (here it is disruption) being achieved by means of the actions (here the actions are 'acting emotions'). You actually fool someone. Pretend fooling doesn't work. The fooling (task) has to be real, the acting fake.

Choose the moment to fool us. Your decision is made because you are an intelligent performer, not a stupid clown.

- PW and HE measure the room, using feet. NP intrudes. There is a physical struggle.

Jon If it's a struggle we need an outcome. Where does the physical struggle take you?

Dragging, pushing, pulling, obstructing a path, avoiding, getting in the way . . .

HE I felt like I got in the way, trying to maintain things.

INTRUDERS 205

Jon   Yes, but if you try and maintain the system, you have to break rules. 'Legalized force.' Do bad things in order to maintain good things. The system works when it's on its own. But when it's tested [by an intruder] it responds like this.

We discuss political systems and whether clowns are the resisters to rules or the totalitarians who do bad things, or both. The students have done a few scenes based on measuring and counting. Counting is the ultimate system.

- OH and TM dance as a couple. HE intrudes by placing herself between them. They throw her out. They try being polite: 'can you just . . . er . . . could you . . . er . . . kind of . . . '. HE leans on them, then holds their feet while they try and dance.

Jon   When you all tried harder, it was funnier. The politeness got tiresome quickly. There are other options, beyond that. If they're dancing, instead of trying to take their place, could you join in by being in a different place. Or when it got vocal, you were shouting, you can use your voice to put them off. Or you could do something completely unrelated to their thing

- A group of three: HD, LS and LH. LH acts as a boss, HD as a runner, LS as a constructor. LH gives both of them instructions. SP enters as intruder and stands in front of them, tries to remove objects, but also obeys LH faster than HD does. LH: 'Who ARE you?' SP repeats her question, mocks LH. SP steals a shoe, LS chases.

Jon   The downstage position for the clown says 'this is just a backdrop for me'. It's a good place to be. Or, you can upstage them! Also a good place to be!

Important, remember to be with us, reminds us that you're in a different world, you're in a different performing mode to them. If you go right into their world, into their fourth wall fantasy, you may still be silly, a fool, a servant, a character, but you will be assimilated. The boss got involved more with the clown, which makes sense. She thought, oh, do I have another worker here? Or the servant and clown could work together, remaining in their modes. [The clown is in a different mode, while the servant, or here the constructor, is in the fictional world.]

206 THE CLOWNING WORKBOOK

We start to work with pieces they already know from other work on their course.

HE, PW and LS begin a performance of something they remember having done previously. It involves a lot of mime. They start disagreeing about 'where the door is'! Some of the students laugh when they recognize the piece the three are trying to reproduce. This is a kind of 'in-joke' clowning. Which is fine, as long as you remember that any outsiders won't get the joke. In-joke clowning happens a lot in our day-to-day social encounters. HD intrudes. She has a stomping loud tone, wrong for their light, high pitched one. While the actors inhabit virtual spaces, HD's mode is human, based on wanting to connect with them through empathy, attempting to understand, to be with them. Their performance mode is cool, abstracted. It's actually a perfect contrast for clowning to emerge. Then suddenly the performers switch mode and sing. HD sings, too, but 'Happy Birthday'.

HD   'No, don't do it, it's dangerous!'

HD follows HE.

HD   'Is this the bit where we . . .?'

PW   'I want to go home!'

HD   'Oh, OK, shall we all go together?'

HD sets out a line of chairs. They get emotional.

HD   'Oh this is my favourite bit.'

Often HD stops and stands and just looks, waiting to understand and then reacts. At the end:

HD   'I think that went really well!'

We applaud.

Jon   I think it went really well, as well! You did a big range of things, as well, joining in, getting it wrong, getting in the way, banality, bringing it back down to earth, wrong performance style, literalness, and always positive. Or responding to sadness, then dropping it. How did you feel being in all that?

HD   Good fun. It was the literalness, the opposite of trying to do a gag.

Jon You have these people doing complex stuff. You can stand back and watch, it gives you time.

HD Because they were detailed and ceremonious, very varied, with noises.

Jon You hadn't seen it?

HD No

Others We did a performance in our placement with a huge group, with people missing now.

Jon Was it inspired in anything particular, or a method of devising?

HE Disconnected objects, associative stuff. 45 minutes. Ten performers.

Jon Imagine if you had 45 mins and ten performers, ask yourself, how would the clown be in that time? Would they go home and come back after having a bath? Would we want you there all the time? Or some? What's the balance?

TM I did see that performance originally and now seeing it 'out of context' . . . what would happen if in every play you went to watch, you got someone intruding. [everyone laughs with joy]

All What a great idea!

Jon What we saw was already a bit wrong, decayed.

TM This is different to just counting as a task. She has to be here with that voice, at that time . . . With that style of acting.

- OH and TM perform a piece with detailed repetitive mime with French text. LH intrudes. She sits at the computer they are using and sings a pop song. The contrast in tone is huge. The abstract versus the sentimental. Oddly, their piece does then move to a tacky bit of music and choreography! LH joins in but as the soloist. LH: 'Oh it's exhausting!' She turns their music off. They try and continue dancing. LH: 'OK, this is a goodie, I think you'll enjoy this.' They go back to the text from the beginning but with LH's song now playing.

HD Wonderful bits when the clown gives distance and comments and refers back to the audience.

Jon   Their world became non-mechanized, but could LH become mechanized to contrast?

The music became the tool by which LH could direct and disrupt things. Turning it off, changing it. It was a great music video. It had that fun quality to it. How was it for you two doing the piece?

OH and **TM**   We could have spent hours building some massive pinata then someone comes on and destroys it. which reminds me how we made the piece. We build a machine then it gets changed/broken. So this reminds me of that.

Jon   It's not surprising that a piece would have built into it something like disruption. It's basic to creation.

19
CLOWNS IN PLAYS

In exploring the dynamic play between the planned and the performed we have used simple plans devised in a few minutes and also more complex organized pieces created outside of the clown workshop. We have also touched on clown drama itself. But what of those scripts which already contain both the clowns and the non-clowns? How can we approach texts that seem to script the clowning, albeit where the clown role seems sparsely detailed?

In this section we will look at the particular case of Shakespeare from the point of view of staging the clowning. To do so we will go directly to a case study.

CASE STUDY 19.1

Clowning and Shakespeare, Drama School – Estonian Academy of Music and Theatre / Rose Bruford College, February 2020

We explored clowning for one week with visiting students from Estonia, as part of their six-week 'Exploring Shakespeare' course. The clowning was surrounded and contextualized by studies on scenes, voice, song, monologues and movement.

Students were asked to familiarize themselves with:

Two Gentlemen of Verona, Act II, Scene 3 (Launce's monologue);

Hamlet, Act III, Scene 2 (The Players and Hamlet);

Midsummer Night's Dream, Act V, Scene 1 (Mechanicals' performance);

Plus the clown scenes in *The Famous Victories of Henry the Fifth* including the whole of Scene 2.

The aim was to address the practical problems of staging clowning in these texts, which span the careers of three of the most influential clowns from the late sixteenth and early seventeenth centuries: Richard Tarlton, Will Kemp and Robert Armin.

19.1 Richard Tarlton

Preparatory exercises

In order to have some tools to attempt this, we first covered some basic laughter response exercises and the intruder exercises:

- experiencing how to work in a dynamic conversation with the audience as a clown responding to laughter;
- breaking the actor's circle of awareness;
- existing in the dual world of the performer, the fiction onstage and the reality of the auditorium.

We then worked on plans and intruders:

- exploring how clowns and non-clown actors co-exist in their contrasting performing modes.

We then turned our full attention to the problem of producing clowning from the texts.

Read and analyze the text

- In pairs or small groups, read Scene 2 of *The Famous Victories of Henry the Fifth*.[1]
- As a whole group, discuss and clarify any questions of language comprehension.

Scene 2 begins with three 'neighbours' (*John Cobbler, Robin Pewterer, Lawrence Costermonger*) gossiping about the Prince and whether he is a thief

CLOWNS IN PLAYS

and if so if his father will not let him be King. These are characters from the lower classes and seem somewhat comic, but they are not clowns in the performative sense. It is midnight and whilst one leaves, the other two sit down to sleep, though wary of danger.

We then have the following sequence, which is what will interest us most here:

Enter Derrick roving.
Derrick Whoa! whoa there! whoa there!
Exit Derrick.
Enter Robin.
Robin O neighbours, what mean you to sleep, and such ado in the streets?
John and Lawrence How now, neighbour, what's the matter?
Enter Derrick again.
Derrick Whoa there! whoa there! whoa there!
John Why, what ail'st thou? Here is no horses.
Derrick Oh, alas, man, I am robbed! Whoa there, whoa there!
Robin Hold him, neighbour Cobbler.
John seizes Derrick.
Why, I see thou art a plain clown.
Derrick Am I a clown? Zounds, masters, do clowns go in silk apparel? I am sure all we gentlemen clowns in Kent scant go so well. Zounds, you know clowns very well.

Following that, there is an encounter with a thief and a boy who tells the neighbours of wild goings on amongst the Prince's entourage.

The text might look obscure, and probably not very funny, so it's worth taking time to clarify. If we can do that with students whose first language is not even modern English, I think it's worth the effort. But just understanding the words won't yet reveal its funniness. How then, can we analyze it so that it works in practice?

First staging

- Stage it, as a plan.
- Divide the action up into simple steps (as in the Step-Laugh exercise with scripts).
- Dialogue can be paraphrased approximation to the original.

212   THE CLOWNING WORKBOOK

There are 16 or so students, in groups of three or four, so we get to see four or five versions.

Second staging

- Re-stage the scene, but remove the clown role of Derrick.
- Rewrite as necessary in order to make sense.

Again we benefit from seeing several ways of conceiving of the scene without a clown.

Third staging

- Repeat the previous staging.
- Add an intruder.
- The intruder must elicit laughter.
- The actors can only go on (one 'step') when we laugh because of the intruder.
- The intruder can use ANY means to elicit laughter.

At this stage, the intruder draws on the earlier exercises with the multiple intruder options that they presented. There is no need to narrow things down to the original at this point.

Fourth staging

- Repeat the second staging again.
- Plus an intruder.
- The intruder uses bits of the original text in order to elicit laughter.

Some outcomes:

- The first group presents their clown-less version for the second time, HM as the intruder begins by pulling up a trouser leg, his gaze on the audience, urging us to find him funny. At some point we laugh. The actors deliver lines of greeting to each other as 'neighbours'. The

CLOWNS IN PLAYS

213

> intruder looks to us, seemingly not knowing what to do, but also apparently comfortable in the flop. We laugh again. The actors continue, with a question, the intruder snaps his fingers to get our attention and some of us laugh, the actors answer the question. The intruder tries wobbling his hands in an odd way, this gets a laugh. The actors speak of thieves. The intruder points at a spectator as if to say 'laugh'. We laugh. The actors look to stage left, where the thief will enter from. The intruder imitates a horse sound, we laugh and the thief enters. The intruder continues to look for potential laughing spectators and then focuses on them until they laugh.

This strategy relies heavily on a constant contact with the audience. More than 'asides', it places the clown and audience in the same world, looking in on the actors' world. This kind for clown feels like the 'audience onstage', or the audience's point of view.

With another group, the intruder seems to have a different status and it almost feels like it's this clown person who is running this show, who is directing it. The clown can seem to be an outsider if they merely commentate, from a distance. On the other hand, it can seem as if the clown takes ownership. How was this effect achieved? Once you realize you have control over when the actors may continue, you can exert your control:

- Experiment with starting and stopping the action at will (by choosing not to be funny).

In order to explore more freely what the clowns could do, we now repeat the scenes with a free-form clown intruder, but this time the clown speaks their own language (here, Estonian), whilst the non-clown actors remain in English. This not only allows for more inventiveness in the clowns, but also makes the divide between clowns and non-clowns even more obvious. Given that the audience in the workshop is 95% Estonian, the clown now should feel even more 'one of us' (excluding me!).

- MAJ begins intruding with an introductory speech, she stays distant from the audience and the other actors, but because she has the 'floor' she can speak what she wants, as long as she wants. The clown owns

214 THE CLOWNING WORKBOOK

the stage, perhaps on behalf of the audience. In contrast, the actors feel like little puppets in a story – which is no bad thing! This kind of clown is certainly akin to a storyteller, or maybe a puppeteer, but although she has power of the proceedings, there is always a certain alienation between clown and actors/story, they are never quite unified. Again, this is a source of pleasure for the audience.

Jon OK, tell me about the clown here.

They explain what she was saying.

Jon You have the language of the audience and the language of 'somewhere else'. You could do the performance in Latin, or . . . in sixteenth century English!

Jon As the intruding clown, try and take control. Not involved, with no responsibility.

- Another group. AMK as the clown makes a grand gesture to indicate the space is his. We laugh. The actors act. AMK is now doubtful. We laugh, the actors act. His attempts to assert control flop, so we laugh and the story goes on. This clown is fun for us, since he has failed to dominate.

Next, we try to introduce some of the elements of the original text, from the role of Derrick.

Use them when you want, randomly, you have the horse, an accusation, the clothes he's wearing and so on. Keep the clown in Estonian for now. It's your show, clown.

- ME as the next clown is also doubtful, awkward. At first she seems more concerned with getting the actors' attention than with us in the audience. By focusing eye contact on the actors, the clown seems to disappear into their world and leave ours. Only when the awkwardness is shared with us do we engage and laugh.

Next, we re-write the staging in order to re-insert the role of Derrick fully. Then they perform again, with Derrick doing the things that Derrick is supposed to do (according to the text), but the action only proceeds when we laugh. The

CLOWNS IN PLAYS

clown can now use both languages, English when interacting with the non-clowns, and Estonian when addressing the audience.

- JKM, the intruder clown arrives on a mimed horse and plays with the sound until we laugh. The actors begin. Playing Derrick, he looks for his horse in a clearly fake way. We laugh. They go on. He asks us the audience if we think he is a clown. We laugh. He switches from English to Estonian. The actors continue to dialogue between themselves and the clown directs all his words to us in the audience. Most of the clown's subsequent actions are reactions in sound and gesture to the actors.

Jon It's rough, but yes, that's how it should look, that's it. That's how it should feel, here is this crazy clown guy who is making this show happen, and he's in it and he's not in it and it's ridiculous and they're telling a story, which we get, but there are two modes. He's running the show but he's 'oh what are they doing?' you're in and you're out. Good.

This is the point when we could start to rehearse, now we understand how it works, now you could start to rehearse what you do, what you are saying. This is just the beginning.

- The next group have an intruder clown who takes over the downstage area to show off his ridiculous horse moves, leaving the actors to occupy upstage for the story. This literally separates them from the audience, which emphasizes our relationship with the clown. ERS continues downstage and makes negative comments about the actors for our amusement. He overdoes it, swears then apologizes. His thoughts go off in tangents, which is fun. It has the makings of a rambling stand-up monologue of sorts.

We now have a first attempt at a method to produce rough versions of performance where the clowns are actually funny whilst the actors get on with the play. Rather than a flat, homogenous set of comic characters which fail to jump out at us on the stage, we have a dynamic play between two modes of performance. And we can start to see, feel and understand what kind of a clown might be traced here.

19.2 Will Kemp

Preparatory exercise: enter when you feel funny

As with the work on Tarlton, we begin by preparing ourselves for a solo entrance. To do so, we use exercises which require the solo performer to enter the stage when they feel funny/stupid and to exit the stage when this feeling isn't there. When onstage, you must advance with your planned monologue.

Read and analyze the text

- As a group, sit and read Launce's monologue (*Two Gentlemen of Verona* Act II, Scene 3).
- Discuss and clarify any questions of language comprehension.

Here is the text extract:

Enter LAUNCE, leading a dog
LAUNCE
Nay, 'twill be this hour ere I have done weeping;
all the kind of the Launces have this very fault. I
have received my proportion, like the prodigious
son, and am going with Sir Proteus to the Imperial's
court. I think Crab, my dog, be the sourest-natured
dog that lives: my mother weeping, my father
wailing, my sister crying, our maid howling, our cat
wringing her hands, and all our house in a great
perplexity, yet did not this cruel-hearted cur shed
one tear: he is a stone, a very pebble stone, and
has no more pity in him than a dog: a Jew would have
wept to have seen our parting; why, my grandam,
having no eyes, look you, wept herself blind at my
parting. Nay, I'll show you the manner of it. This
shoe is my father: no, this left shoe is my father:
no, no, this left shoe is my mother: nay, that
cannot be so neither: yes, it is so, it is so, it
hath the worser sole. This shoe, with the hole in

CLOWNS IN PLAYS

it, is my mother, and this my father; a vengeance
on't! there 'tis: now, sit, this staff is my
sister, for, look you, she is as white as a lily and
as small as a wand: this hat is Nan, our maid: I
am the dog: no, the dog is himself, and I am the
dog – Oh! the dog is me, and I am myself; ay, so,
so. Now come I to my father; Father, your blessing:
now should not the shoe speak a word for weeping:
now should I kiss my father; well, he weeps on. Now
come I to my mother: O, that she could speak now
like a wood woman! Well, I kiss her; why, there
'tis; here's my mother's breath up and down. Now
come I to my sister; mark the moan she makes. Now
the dog all this while sheds not a tear nor speaks a
word; but see how I lay the dust with my tears.

We are going to work with the students' own language the whole time on
this text, so:

- In pairs, make a written translation of the text (it can be accurate or just
  from memory).
- If your first language is English, try making a modern transcription using
  your own kind of language – if you speak a dialect of English, use it![2]

First staging – sharing versions

We now see what a first attempt to put these new versions on a stage looks like:

- One person takes the stage with their script in hand and delivers it
  however they wish.
- It can be a simple reading (but standing up) or include some attempt to
  physicalize the action, it doesn't matter at this stage.
- Then one person from each of the pairs, in turn, until we have had one
  version of each text. They may resemble each other nearly completely,
  or not, it doesn't matter.

Even with these simple readings there is some laughter already.

Second staging – only when you feel funny

We now apply directly the preparatory exercise of entering with the feeling of funny/stupid:

- Begin backstage.
- When you feel funny/stupid and the pleasure to enter, come on and use your text.
- When the feeling goes, leave the stage.
- And so on until the monologue is over.

The other person in each pair takes the stage in turn.

- The first actor tries. KK cautiously looks out and we giggle so he approaches centre stage and speaks a little, then realizes we are not responding, pauses and leaves, but then we laugh because he has realized we didn't laugh, so he comes back and continues, again to our laughs, because he thinks we like what he did. After a while, the same pattern: he suddenly realizes he's lost us, turns to leave and we laugh. He next cuts his own speech in the middle when he realizes and goes. He returns looking very smug, which we laugh at. He pauses and loses his place in the monologue, so we laugh.

In this case, he has identified his own self-feeling stupid with our laughter, which is fine. Perhaps our laughing at him was what always provoked this feeling in him, which is quite normal.

We comment on how it went.

MES It revitalized it every time that he reappeared. Then it died out, and he knew that.

KK It's hard to keep the attention, because the monologue is so lively, because he plays with the shoes and the dog, and then the focus goes, he's making this world happen in front of our eyes, so you have to really be inside it to make it feel like it's there. But if you're repeating what the text says, almost every sentence ends with a 'I should go now . . .'

Jon Yes, that's fine for now.

CLOWNS IN PLAYS

- The next actor KK is offstage and blows his nose loudly. No reaction. He sighs. Coughs. Nothing. He enters. It seems his pleasure is low. When questioned on that, KK shows he realizes he wasn't doing the exercise right, and feels stupid. We laugh. He continues, energized. We can see how he feels being onstage in front of us. He now looks disappointed, and exits. We laugh and he returns with the feeling from before. This pattern repeats several times. Every time he picks up the shoes he is playing with and leaves, we sense a strong feeling and laugh and so he returns.

Jon Did you notice that you when you were leaving and when you came back it was the same time that we laughed?

KK Yeah, yeah, yeah.

Jon Were you doing that because you heard the laugh or because that's when you have the feeling?

KK I kind of reacted because of the laugh, and it was a good feeling.

Jon OK, perfect, that's exactly right. So now we will say always that you come back when you have the feeling or when we laugh. It can be the same thing.

Spectator 1 It was best when he was confused.

Spectator 2 Yes, he was very sensitive to when was the right time to leave.

Jon Yes, it is very different to come up here and think 'I'm doing my acting, I'm going to act' to taking your time to feel 'OK, I'm here first.' So, be careful, we have a tiny studio here, and you don't have to be good [at acting] . . . Yet.

What you said was the problem – with not knowing it by heart – becomes a little bit your help. It brings you back to here. Because this problem brings you to the reality of the auditorium – you have your new text [in your hand] and you have your audience. This is a problem that only you can solve. 'Launce' the character cannot solve this. It's not a character thing, it's a clown thing.

In fact, that is what the problem of the actor is. Traditionally the actor and the writer are two different people. The writer, the playwright, writes the words which the actor will speak. They not only are the words of the character who is not you, they are the words written by another. So how do you meet these words? Here you have this problem. How do you bring alive something which you have not thought of?

- HA enters in a lively manner, as if planned, but is it convincing? When questioned, feelings rise to the surface. Now he returns with a smile. Then he wants to exit when laughing at himself. But no, this is pleasure, to stay! He leaves, rather slowly, which is nearly amusing. He jumps back on, maybe not convincing, then loses his way with the text and then we laugh. Again he gets lost and we laugh. And again. Now he gets so lost that he leaves the stage. We laugh a little from offstage he laughs and so do we and he enters. Lost again. Laughs. Now he speaks whilst retaining that pleasure at being lost. Next time he gets lost he doesn't look at his text but instead looks up at us, his face smiling and stupid. The next attempted entrance, with an unconvincing pleasure, makes him laugh as soon as he arrives.

The actor who can't remember his text is good to watch! And when his feeling at not remembering becomes his overriding feeling while performing, the performance is good to watch, too.

MES I think it's a bit different for him, it's hard for him to find the feeling to NOT want to be onstage. In a good way.

Jon Yes, he always wants to be onstage.

MES It looks like he's always having enjoyment, so he has to find a way to go backstage.

Jon Yes, you went backstage like this [tries to imitate his focus]. It's full of pleasure, you should be ON stage.

The next actor gets up.

Jon Already you have pleasure, we can see it [before she has begun].

- MK begins and soon, for some reason, laughs at what she is doing and saying. We join in the laughter. She 'controls' herself and continues. Again, the same pattern, the laugh escapes, we join, she controls. Eventually she leaves, it feels like a good moment to pause.

CLOWNS IN PLAYS

> Backstage, she and we laugh and she returns swiftly in a way that makes us laugh more. And herself. Then she leaves when we laugh, which is contrary, but still right. Then remembers and returns. Silence now and she leaves. Backstage, the silence seems funny and she comes back. And so on. Again she wants to leave when she fails to get her text right and feels stupid and we laugh, but this is when we want her to stay, which she remembers just after.

Spectator 1 It looked like she went backstage to read, to remember the lines.

Actor It made me feel uncomfortable.

Jon Yes, this is a strong feeling, a stage feeling. So you can have the stage feeling of 'I don't know the lines', and that is the feeling which will energize whatever you have to portray. You can use any feeling which is real to fill this fictional character, so it's your raw energy which you have – the real person – has. And the clown can have those feelings are about 'oh I forget, I'm stupid, I can't do it'. This feeling you have here when you leave, it's very strong, and it makes us feel you are here, so we see you. It's a negative. This is a little bit about what I said before about encouraging each other to be bad because that's when we see you.

Third staging – try harder

- At some point from now you can get rid of the script and just remember what you remember.

- This time, when onstage and your pleasure goes, do something to bring it back rather than exiting.

- Two possible things you can try at this point:

  1 Sing.
  2 Dance.

- Then, when the feeling stupid/funny pleasure comes back, go back to your script.

If you hate singing or dancing, you also have that problem of another 'bad' feeling. You can use that, too.

Two reasons:

1 Singing and dancing are commonly held to generate pleasure and they are something you can do alone.

2 Will Kemp was a singer/dancer.[3]

• The next actor enters. When MES's pleasure goes, he pauses, seeming to know and maybe fear what he has to do next. He starts to hum and then sing and we laugh quickly. Again, he stops when the pleasure goes and the pause seems to generate the laugh almost before he sings. When he does get to sing, the tone dies and the feeling of flopping seems to reach us directly through the voice. But then he sings and does a little dance which makes us and him laugh but then he goes towards the exit. As if the floppy feeling was a reason to go, not stay. Again, but this time we call him back.

Jon Good. You had the pleasure, then the text, then it goes, then it's like you don't have any feeling, then you do your singing and dancing, then the feeling comes back because you feel stupid, and then you do your text. You went from pleasure to blocked to singing to feeling. So the singing was your solution for the problem from before [being blocked].

• Next actor. MS sings for herself offstage, as if to get ready. We laugh, and she enters. Her pleasure goes, she pauses, and then sings with an accompanying dance, feels stupid and continues. The song and dance bits get longer, continuing even when she has found the funny feeling that should send her back to her script. Then sometimes the script comes back as if on top of this feeling generated by the song and dance.

MS It's hard to believe how fun it is.

Jon I think you were using the singing and dancing when you were getting near to the bad feeling.

MS Yes, yes.

CLOWNS IN PLAYS

Jon   But the bad feeling is still the pleasure, so you could have stayed with that. Sometimes you used the singing and dancing to get away from that, to get to 'ah, now I'm okay!' And then you go back to 'oh shit!' Which is great, also.

Remember, Kemp was famous for being a solo performer who could be on the stage, and entertaining people with no need for the plot or the story or anyone else. So it's even more separate from what we looked at yesterday [Tarlton]. So it's normal and easy to make his speeches into a little bit of a show. If you have another thing that brings you this fun, you could put it in here. If you like to tell a joke, or you could do a magic trick. Why not? We're just playing with it at the moment.

With more attempts, the group can learn from each other and gradually experiment with bringing together the stage feelings and script.

MES   JTK kept the energy up all the time.

Jon   Yeah, that was good.

MES   Because then my attention is also with him. Even when he went down, there was the same attention. There was like no difference between them.

Also, the script becomes more and more familiar and they are able to play off-book.

Fourth staging – off-book

Jon   You have plenty to play with: you have the singing, you have the dancing and you have your memory and you have the pleasure and you have the stage and you have your audience. What more could you want? And remember you have the props, a hat, the shoes, the dog . . . Now it's showtime.

- HA tries. He has lots of resources which he draws on to keep us amused and manages to keep it this enmeshed in the script as far as he remembers.

Jon   Whoa, what's your feeling?

MES   I feel he's feeling so cool, but I don't want to be in his skin at all. [everyone laughs]

Jon   Yes! It's like 'aargh!' It's a cringe.

MES   Yes!

Jon   That's good. This cringe. That's good. Yeah, this is crazy. So, this is the clown that's funny because they think they're funny. It's good. This is what you have. The way we can love you. And this is the part of the clown which is a little bit annoying. It's what you've got! Remember when we talked earlier about, maybe some people in the group find this easier? You said that because you don't care so much about being comic? But for those that it [being comic] is important for them, it is a struggle sometimes. But in the end, you have your way.

Spectator 1   I think that just watching each other like that brings us to our relationship [as friends and classmates].

Jon   Now you just need to find yourself a company who wants to play all the other characters and you say, 'I'll come in and do that bit with the dog, don't worry about it, it'll be funny'. And they say 'great because we don't have anyone who's funny'. So you turn up and do your bit and get paid and go home. That's it, you're a solo clown.

Is this what Kemp looked and felt like? Obviously we have no idea, and in any case we aren't trying to reproduce something. Certainly it's now funny, subtle, playful, engaging and alive! What more could you hope for from a modern-day rendering of Shakespeare's clowns?

What next?

The clowns of Tarlton and Kemp stand right at the dawn of the early modern stage in England. It could be argued that Tarlton WAS the dawn of the early modern theatre. Now that we have some practical method to work with this material, we can go on to consider further developments in clowning in Shakespeare, and beyond. At least we have a background, which is founded in practice and also in some of what we know of clown history (which is a very different perspective to an analysis which comes from literature studies, for example). Armin

CLOWNS IN PLAYS

(the clown brought into the world of the fiction), and *Hamlet* (the play with no clown performer) are surely better explored if we assume that the more 'separated' styles of Tarlton and Kemp were the foundation of the genre, which new developments in clowning could later depart from or build upon.

NOTES

Preface

1 Gaulier's claim that there are 'only three clowns' in the world at any one time (Gaulier 2015).

2 Stanislavski's recent biographer and translator, Jean Benedetti: 'Had Stanislavski been a "natural", had his talent – some would say his genius – as an actor found an immediate, spontaneous outlet, there would be no "system". As it was, it took years of persistent, unrelenting effort to remove the blocks and barriers which inhibited the free expression of his great gifts. His search for the "grammar" of acting was the result of that struggle. What we receive as the "system" originated from his attempt to analyze and monitor his own progress as an artist and his attempts to achieve his ideas as an actor and meet his developing standards, and it is all the more valuable for being born of concrete activity since the solutions he found were lived and not the result of speculation or abstract theory.' (2008: 1–2)

3 Lecoq's writings on clown (and bouffon) reveal just how little 'outcome' we have from what, to all intents and purposes, were experiments based on asking simple questions. Those who were present at the beginnings of those experiments will attest to just how little this work resembled a 'system'.

Introduction

1 'Clowns first appeared in the 1960s, when I was investigating the relationship between the commedia dell'arte and circus clowns. My main discovery came in answer to a simple question: the clown makes us laugh, but how? One day I suggested that the students should arrange themselves in a circle – recalling the circus ring – and make us laugh. One after the other, they tumbled, fooled around, tried out puns, each one more fanciful than the one before, but in vain! The result was catastrophic.' (Lecoq 2000: 152–54)

2 At the First Studio, which Stanislavski founded in 1912, and which nurtured a group of young actors and directors who were to become the leading teachers of acting for the next forty years, there was a large book, left permanently on display, in which the members could write down suggestions for exercises and improvisations. It was freely used. The vitality of the First Studio lay in its willingness to experiment. That is an example worth following. (Benedetti 1998: 15)

3 Konijn records that 'During monologues the heartrate reached extremes of 180 beats per minute' (1997: 109), compared to a rest rate of 60 bpm, or a rate of 140 bpm when someone does an extreme activity like parachuting.

1 Introductions and warm-ups

1 The lineage of post-war ensemble practices is a rich and complex one, encompassing the Viewpoints theory developed in the 1970s by choreographer Mary Overlie and the exercises adapted by Anne Bogart for actors (see, for example, the instruction to 'notice how even the space is' (Bogart 2004: 44)). The ensemble approach bore heavily on the development of Lecoq's method (see, for example, his 'plateau' exercise, where the chorus balance the hero's movements (Evans and Kemp 2016: 153–54), as well as more politically motivated performance collectives over several decades. It also formed a core value in the evolution of improvisation in theatre (see, for example, Viola Spolin's 'space substance' exercises, where 'players move around and physically investigate space as an unknown substance' (Spolin 1973: 80–82) and in the new bebop style of jazz, which produced a 'framework of spontaneous egalitarian interaction' (Belgrad 1998: 191)). The rise to prominence of ensemble approaches in the late twentieth century is not an isolated phenomenon, of course, and its own theatrical genealogy may be traced in early twentieth century practitioners such as Copeau, Meyerhold and Michael Chekhov.

2 For an earlier discussion of the issue of warm-ups for clown training, see Davison 2015: 'Do clowns warm-up? [. . .] Despite the weight of orthodoxy, I felt forced to observe that playing lots of theatre and other games won't automatically make you into a clown.' (Davison 2015: 9)

3 The practice of reflecting via the 'I liked . . .' construction probably arises from a desire to foreground the subjectivity of the observer as well as emphasizing the positive 'constructive' mode of criticism. Although now well-established, even orthodox, it is frequently challenged by trainers searching for a radical reflexivity that distances the observer from their own habitual reactions. See, for example, Daniel Banks' 'The Hip Hop Initiative:

NOTES 229

We the Griot': 'I ask the group "What did you see?" (If they fall into the habit of saying "I liked" or "I didn't like", I bring them back to "I saw . . .")'. (Luckett and Shaffer 2017: 157)

4 'This is improvisation. The First Amendment in action. This is the story of that proliferation, of improv comedy's fifty-year ascent [. . .] to philosophy of being – and all of it as American as democracy. For improvisation isn't merely an analogue for democracy, it is democracy, demanding that its individual players and audience members uphold the democratic ideal of total collaboration, of hearing and being heard, and rewarding both sides with the very good feeling of shared humanity.' (Wasson 2017: xii–xiii)

5 'One of the main attributes of the medieval clown was precisely the transfer of every high ceremonial gesture or ritual to the material sphere; such was the clown's role during tournaments, the knight's initiation, and so forth. It is in this tradition of grotesque realism that we find the source of the scenes in which Don Quixote degrades chivalry and ceremonial.' (Bakhtin 1984: 20)

6 Meisner again: 'So you're going to be nervous! Be nervous! Did you ever hear that line – every actor knows it – "I thought I'd die until I got my first laugh!" You follow? The first laugh means "We love you".' (Meisner 1987: 176)

2 Name Tag

1 Benedetti on Stanislavski's coining of the present tense verb 'to be': 'This is a case of Stanislavski inventing or rather reviving a lost word. The verb to be only exists in Russian in the infinitive, "est". Stanislavski uses the first person singular, "ja esm", which no one would normally use. "I am being" is a way of conveying his usual usage.' (1998: 6)

2 'The Game allows things which are unbelievable and marvellous, not feelings. Enjoy pretending to feel, without feeling. The pleasure of lying will give your lies the appearance of truth. You will be believed. Theatre lives off this "lying truth". Why don't you feel anything? To liberate the joy of pretending, so you will not be soiled by truth. People who look for the real truth in the theatre, rather than the not-real truth, are fanatical preachers and true (not pretend) arseholes. What a shame! The truth kills the joy of imagining.' (2007a: 196)

3 'Since finite games can be played within an infinite game, infinite players do not eschew the performed roles of finite play. On the contrary, they enter finite games with all the appropriate energy and self-veiling, but they do so without the seriousness of finite players.' (Carse 1986: 18)

4 A deduction made frequently by clown trainers and students since Lecoq that the witnessing of a performer's failures in front of an audience is an indication that the 'truth' has been revealed having removed the 'masks' which 'conceal' this authentic self which lies behind it.

3 Ball play

1 See Davison 2015: 27-32.

2 Luckett and Shaffer describe the Hendricks Method in these terms: 'In line with Afrocentricity, the methodology is purposefully infused with verbal and physical acts of positivity, such as uplifting speeches, pats on the back, or compliments about appearance and talent. This type of positivity is crucial for minorities, as they encounter a certain set of experiences that include discrimination and prejudices at a very young age.' (2017: 20–21)

3 Patch Adams often speaks about how he considers his job not primarily to make someone laugh, but to make contact, or connection. His mission would be to seek out people who appear 'disconnected', which he defines in a simple manner: someone who is alone and not engaged in eye contact with another person. The job is to find the way to make eye contact with that person and ideally share a smile. For Adams, this equates to reconnecting that person not just with himself, but with humanity as a whole. (Adams 2007)

4 Much of the recording of these sessions was done in audio only, for reasons of group consent, which proved to be unexpectedly revealing. What listening to those audio tracks later, for the purposes of this book, brought into focus was how the acoustic information is more than sufficient for us to recognize such things as when someone is acting habitually, or surprisingly, or is being affected by other players, or even when they are looking at the audience or not. Although bearing in mind, of course, that I knew exactly what was happening visually, given that I have done these exercises many times.

5 Over the period 2007–2010, when I worked as a full-time researcher at RCSSD investigating clown/actor training, I had the privilege to be able to teach on all but two of the BA and MA courses at the school, such as: BA Drama, Applied Theatre and Education, BA Theatre Practice, BA Acting, MA Classical Acting, MA Acting for Screen, MA Actor Training and Coaching, MA Applied Theatre, MA Theatre Studies, MA Voice Studies, MA Writing for Stage and Broadcast Media and MA Performance Practice and Research. Each course and its cohort and staff had their own concerns and priorities, which clown training was able to address from the starting point of a stable yet flexible approach. Each course contributed insights which only such specialization could have brought about.

4 Doing things when it's funny

1 As far as I can recall, from notes and memory, this must have first been tried in a group in Spring 2017 at London Clown School, but didn't give spectacular results. It was then re-tested at the research workshops at Rose Bruford College in September 2017, as something 'new'. It began to take off with the new intake at London Clown School in Autumn 2017, a large, diverse and energetic group that were particularly hungry to find out how clowning happens. Indeed, much of the impetus for a large part of the training presented in this book, was given birth during those classes.

2 Keith Johnstone listed a number of strategies to avoid in improvisation. Some of his advice is useful for clowning (though some of it isn't, obviously, as these are two distinct genres). Amongst the many 'don'ts' that Keith Johnstone identified for improvisers to avoid, was what he termed 'joining' (copying another performer's activity) and 'agreed activities': 'Having the same reaction as your partner is a way to avoid tilting the balance. [. . .] Never accept joining as proof that the players are working well together.' (1999: 118) 'Little Red and the wolf play hide-and-seek and spin-the-turtle; and then they practise ballroom dancing. The characters seem to be working well together, but no one is in trouble, and no one is being altered (except for the turtle).' (1999: 120)

3 'Meisner believes that action is not in the character or the plot of the play but in relationships. To this end he stresses the repetition exercise, because the exercise compels the actor to "work off the partner". In this way the partner allows the actor to create the role from the given material present on stage and in the life of another person, rather than a mental preconception of character. Meisner's repetition exercise, as opposed to Adler's emphasis on circumstances, is intended to promote impulsive behaviour as a consequence of living relationships (the actual moment on stage), rather than merely the given situation. The repetition exercise is used to read behaviour either from the scene-partner or the spectators. In direct address, the actor's attention is not, as Worthen implies, "diverted from the audience"; rather, the audience should be viewed as the scene-partner. In other words, in directly addressing the audience the actor uses the audience in much the same way as a stand-up comic does: gauging the laughter and responses of the spectators and responding according to the actor's impulses.' (Krasner, in Hodge 2010: 146)

4 Vasudevi Reddy's theories about infant humour posit a model where laughter is elicited through interactive dynamics between babies and adults, rather than through cognitive concepts such as incongruity. She draws explicit parallels between what babies under 12 months do with their parents to what adult clowns do with their audiences. Reddy's work with early years education and child psychology is a distinct break with previous cognitive models, which previously claimed that children only acquired 'humour skills' in parallel with cognitive development. 'Identifying clowning. There are two ways in which one can approach the identification of clowning in everyday interactions: One, through looking for instances where an act which obtains laughter from others is intentionally repeated in order to re-elicit the laughter, i.e. to approach the phenomenon neutral to the content of the act. And two, through looking for similarities with the acts which clowns in many societies are known to do, i.e. focusing on the content of the act, and enabling, for instance, the identification of acts which may only be performed once.' (Reddy 2001: 250)

5 Mamet has consistently argued in favour of material actions being the only ones an actor can, or should be called upon, to act. Anything more abstract is undoable. 'The Method got it wrong. Yes, the actor is undergoing something onstage, but it is beside the point to have him or her "undergo" the supposed trials of the character upon the stage. The actor has his own trials to undergo, and they are right in front of him. They don't have to be superadded; they exist. His challenge is not, to recapitulate, to pretend to the difficulties of the written character; it is to open the mouth, stand straight, and say the words bravely—adding nothing, denying nothing, and without the intent to manipulate anyone: himself, his fellows, the audience. To learn to do that is to learn to act.' (1998: 22)

6 Brussels, November 2019.

5 On/Off

1 Davison 2015: 64–71.

2 It's worth asking ourselves here whether we could also, in a slightly different sense, characterize the spectator's response as 'scripted' or partly conditioned. If we expect to watch a clown performance, for example, we are very probably expecting to laugh (or perhaps expecting to be supposed to laugh but not hopeful of that happening). Either way, the expected responses will be 'laughter' or its absence. If, on the other hand, we are going to watch a melodramatic film, we will expect to have a different set of responses, perhaps to feel angry, to weep, and so on. These sets of expected responses are in part at least determined by the genre and or pre-knowledge of it. We 'learn' how to spectate, through social conditioning. This is clear when we see how children and young adults don't respond 'correctly'. I remember as a teenager at school not being able to stop laughing when opera was played.

6 Step-Laugh

1 'Davison augments a game of Gaulier's in order to teach this skill of replaying scripted material according to spontaneous responses. At Gaulier's school, a line of five students stands on stage. The game is a race to the front of the stage, each student taking a step forward each time the audience laugh at them. [. . .] Using his own teaching experience, Davison argues that the relationship between clown and audience must be honest and original to the moment in which it is performed, but that it is not important whether the material performed is improvised or scripted.' (Amsden 2015: 127)

2 'Step-Laugh builds a relationship based on laughter response, without which there can be no clown. The poetry which some claim for clowns can only come from here, otherwise it's just wishful thinking at best and pure ego at worst. Clowns have nothing to say, to misquote Lecoq, which is where their profundity, if you can call it that, lies. Because there is nothing to say. These at least are the values I perceive behind my own teaching practice. If yours are different then the clown for you will be different too. This is an interpretation of what is going on when a clown flops which is distinct to that which Lecoq himself offered when commenting on that early discovery of the teaching method for clown.' (Davison 2015: 72)

3 My memory is patchy here, but creating this exercise may well have been influenced by Peter Brook's famous dictum with which he begins *The Empty Space*: 'I can take any empty space and call it a bare stage. A man walks across this empty space whilst someone else is watching him, and this is all that is needed for an act of theatre to be engaged.' (Brook 1968: 11) Although Brook's abstract or neutral concept of a supposedly universal theatre is highly questionable, it can serve specific needs in specific circumstances. Such as here.

4 Paul Bouissac theorizes this as one of the fundamental endings for clown action – the staging of exile, the punishment for transgression: 'the transgressor eventually pays for this crime. First he is increasingly at the receiving end of the gags, and finally he is mobbed out of the circus, a metaphor of the circle of civilization. It is symptomatic that some commentators have noted what they consider 'a weak ending' (e.g. Little 1993: 122). Given the magnitude of the transgression, the only logical conclusion would be the killing of the transgressor of lower status, who becomes the scapegoat. In the Pipo and Zavatta interpretation, the death of the auguste is briefly evoked as a last deceptive trick, but the chase soon resumes to exclude the perpetrator from the community. This is indeed a strong ending commensurate with the virtual semiotic crime he has committed.' (Bouissac 2015: 122)

NOTES

5   The realization that the point of the exercise does not depend on whether the material is improvised or scripted is vital. It clarifies one of the areas of confusion that has arisen from the clown-as-play model. The confusion results from the discovery that the flop cannot be scripted, that the clown's relationship with the audience must be created in the moment. It is often then assumed that everything the clown does must be somehow spontaneous, that the audience should see everything coming into creation in the present (Davison 2013: 290–92).

6   The truth is, though, that for me, teaching has always been primarily a way of asking myself questions like 'how does clowning actually work?' rather than an opportunity to 'impart a method' or to 'share a vision'.

7   The oft-cited dogma that runs 'clowns say yes to everything' has established itself as if it had no history, seemingly unchallenged as a 'truth'. Like a large number of these 'truths' in contemporary clowning, it most likely has its historical origins in the range of performance practices that evolved in the post-Second World War period which saw the performer as an individual whose reality lay inside their self or their body, in opposition to the perceived outer-ness of society, convention and inherited culture. This idea that we should free ourselves from social masks is still very entrenched and mostly goes without being questioned.

8   Another, though less fundamental assumption is that of the non-speaking clown. Students and teachers often self-prohibit speaking, though, when questioned why, do not know beyond a vague 'do clowns speak?' Clearly clowns do speak and the idea that one should not speak during a clown exercise is quite clearly absurd.

9   Interestingly, at the beginning of Lecoq's clown experiments, the 'flop' was thought to only occur as a consequence of the 'feat' (a rather poor translation into English of the French 'exploit'). The feat suggests several things in Lecoq's pedagogy, including accidental success, but also implies an attempt. In the case of clowning, this attempt is to make others laugh: 'the core theme had already been identified: clowns make you laugh. So I set up the stage and everyone came on with the sole obligation to make us laugh. It was terrible, ridiculous.' (Lecoq 2006: 114–15)

10 Mark Rylance, reflecting on actors' and directors' experiences in the early days of Shakespeare's Globe in London, spotted, unlike many, that this conversational dynamic is what makes theatre tick. 'I think the Globe building has affected theatre practices more than people want to admit. This architecture does demand much more from an actor. It demands we get over our fear of the audience; that we convince them eye to eye of our reality, that we light our stage with our voices. It gives the audience a different power. Directors who work at the Globe have to dismount their trained circus ponies and learn to ride wild horses. Audiences want to have something more happen than they did twenty years ago. I do not think they

NOTES

235

are happy to sit quietly in the dark and admire us with their minds.' (In Carson and Karim-Cooper 2008: 108)

11 CC: This raises an interesting point; it is the notion of shifting from psychological realism to story-telling. You and the audience are together in a creative process rather than you presenting an artifact to them for appreciation.

MR: Yes, exactly. I think, very quickly, with the first *Winter's Tale* (1997), it became very apparent how vitally important the story was in this space. It was a very beautiful production, but in a few places, it lost the movement of the story, and you could see the audience shifting and wandering. In my five years at the RSC, I had never focused on the story so much. We had focused on finding a certain interpretation of a scene and the director would put together these interpretations into a complete interpretation of the play. In my mind it was a bit like going to see a football match where the two teams had practised an interpretation of the beautiful game. If we went about it that way, rather than actually playing the game, it became apparent very quickly that we were approaching the Globe in the wrong way. We needed to make interpretive choices, but the choices were only how best to serve the story, so it could be played with the audience in one time, one space. They were hungry for the story itself, not a story about the story. [. . .] As I say, many of these things I learned before at the RSC, but the Globe sorted the chaff from the wheat, so to speak. The space told me what was essential and what was just vanity and fashion. (Rylance 2008: 106–08)

12 Preiss cites John Stephens in 1615 who disparaged the 'common player' as one who 'when he doth hold conference upon the stage, and should looke directly in his fellows face, he turns about his voice into the assembly for applause-sake . . . so howsoever hee pretends to have a royall Master or Mistresse, his wages and dependence prove him to be the servant of the people.' (In Preiss 2014: 188)

7 That was/n't funny

1 'Feelings have to be "lured", "enticed". [. . .] it seemed to him that any kind of direct attempt to evoke feeling or the memory of feeling had to be avoided.' (Benedetti 2008: 90)

2 'The actor tries consciously to make things happen, which is in direct contradiction to the processes by which the actions take place in everyday life. The harder you try consciously to achieve, the further you get from allowing natural processes to happen.' (Barker 1977: 44)

3 'The game . . . its immediacy and spontaneity protect the students from false theatricality.' (Evans 2006: 67)

236 NOTES

4 'Such improvisation games have become common in theatre teaching and workshops, and their familiarity has meant that participants are often complacent about such simple well-known games.' (Evans 2006: 129)

5 The notion is, of course, a basic tenet of Romanticism, the artist creating *ex nihilo*.

6 'A present-day literate usually assumes that written records have more force than spoken words as evidence of a long-past state of affairs, especially in court. Earlier cultures that knew literacy but had not so fully interiorized it, have often assumed quite the opposite.' (Ong 1982: 95)

7 See, for example Towsen (1976: 189–205) and Davison (2013: 33–34).

9 Laughter as a pardon

1 'In extreme cases, once you realize that you might be spared punishment even if you don't catch the ball, by making people laugh, then you could opt not even to try and catch it. Someone throws it to you and you don't even raise your hand. The hope is that we will laugh. This risk is to be encouraged and gives us a new range of possibilities in clowning, although it won't work for everyone.' (Davison 2015: 67–68)

2 Davison (2015: 34–38).

10 Conclusion to Part One: Right and wrong thinking

1 The 'Theatre of Failure' lacks this interaction; however, it is essentially an attempt to solve the alienation between spectator and performer inherent in fourth-walled theatre, by means of the mechanics of 'failure = liveness'. See Tannahill: 'It was really the spectre of failure that gave the piece a dramatic charge. There was an irresistible thrill in watching a performer spin a narrative out of thin air knowing full well how easily that story could go awry. The spectre of failure comes from the knowledge that what is unfolding before us is happening live, and thus alive with the possibility that any moment this production, this event, might fall flat on its face.' (2015: 16) It's a good trick, but it still doesn't bridge the gap with an audience, who remains merely 'watching'.

2 'It was like a bright spotlight illuminating what she and the audience were doing in that darkened theatre, all of us fallible mortals grasping at immortal

NOTES 237

questions. A simple cough can surprise an audience, shattering the theatrical illusion.' (Tannahill on Sarah Graton Stanley's 'Failure Theatre: An Artist's Statement' (2015: 17))

3 Aside from genres which are still participatory (some story-telling, some comedy, carnival, and so on), in the West we commonly associate such hyper-interactivity historically with the beginnings of early modern theatre in the late sixteenth century. See, for example, Preiss's study of clowns and authorship: 'Improvising before the crowd is mastery: improvising for them, on the other hand, is the opposite, confessing the material dependence of performance on them, and thus making it a collaborative, unpredictable social event. The need for a "fixed text" was not to censor the clown, but to censor the audience.' (Preiss 2014: 188)

PART TWO 'I FEEL FUNNY'

1 Coburn and Morrison 2013: 42.

11 I (don't) feel funny

1 This idea of the performance of clowning as a dynamic relationship matches what can be observed in infant humour, according to the research of Vasudevi Reddy: 'Humour creation can be seen in these engagements to be an interpersonal rather than individual process. Further, at least in infancy, humour creation is also an emotional rather than primarily intellectual process.' (Reddy 2001: 247)

'Most infants were reported to make others laugh by deliberately repeating actions in order to re-elicit previously obtained laughter. Their actions are compared to actions of adult clowns, showing many similarities and developmental continuities and suggesting that the origins of humour may lie earlier in infancy than hitherto accepted.' (Reddy 2001: 247)

2 'Cry, both of you, then talk. That's my method of acting: cry, then talk. Don't talk and then expect to cry, because you won't!' (Meisner 1987: 199–200)

3 Murray on Lecoq: 'the body (and its movement) produce thought' (2002: 28).

4 Hopefully, I have not (yet) fallen prey to system-makers by trying to force something to fit into the format, rather than changing the format to fit the new discovery. For Lecoq, everything had to be mask-derived. For Stanislavski, everything had to be about 'truth' or 'life'. You can judge my own assumptions for yourself.

5 The most famous example of this might be the 'mistranslations' of Stanislavski's words from Russian to English and their publication in the USA in the early twentieth century. Only in the past ten years have new, 'accurate' translations appeared in English. The 'old versions' gave rise in themselves to a whole new training craze, 'The Method', as practised in the USA and highly influential upon generations of actors on stage and screen, thereby setting trends and orthodox behaviour patterns for actors and their trainers worldwide until the present. See, for example, Benedetti 2008.

6 BA Theatre and Performance Practices, London Metropolitan University, November 2019.

12 Self-laughter

1 See Davison 2013: 200.

2 Davison 2013: 200-04 and Davison 2015: 53–58.

3 On a previous workshop in the same location, on the other hand, the group came from three distinct regions: the two halves of Belgium and also from the Netherlands.

4 The recent commercial expansion of universities from the West into east Asia has included the export of clown training approaches to China in particular, not necessarily on terms beneficial or appropriate to those receiving the training. Cultural colonialism is nothing new, of course. Lecoq admitted that on his visit to Japan to teach, he found students marvellously good at the exercises with set scripts ('Farewell to the Boat', in Lecoq 2000: 41) but confusingly bad at the improvisations. Is this simply a case of the inapplicability of Western-derived elements, and the familiarity of Asian-derived ones? (Lecoq and his predecessors openly borrowed (or appropriated) from Japanese Noh theatre and other Asian forms without inside cultural knowledge.)

5 Some time ago, I became interested in the posture of laughter. That research sought a link with posture when experiencing failure (losing a game, the flop), noting observations such as: 'the head tilts back, sometimes in a wave through the spine; the knees come up, vertically, one at a time, sometimes repeatedly; the stomach draws in; the chest collapses; the eyes open wider than normal; the mouth opens.' (Davison 2008, including images)

14 Guess the show

1 See Davison 2015: 76, 'The Problem of Fiction'.

NOTES 241

6 See Dominique Denis's categorization of clown types which draws on actual performers' personalities (1985: 2–6).

7 See Opie, Iona and Opie, Peter (1969) *Children's Games in Street and Playground*, pp. 129–30. For its potential use in clown training, see Davison 2008, accessed at: http://jondavison.blogspot.com/2008/01/draft-notes-on-contemporary-clown.html

19 Clowns in plays

1 *The Famous Victories of Henry the Fifth* is by an anonymous author. We know that Richard Tarlton, the first performer in history to go by the name of 'Clown', played the role of Derrick. The first published edition is from 1598, ten years after his death. Tarlton's legacy is the context for most of the clowning in plays during the following half century, including, of course, those who worked in Shakespeare's company. The text is available free online: https://internetshakespeare.uvic.ca/doc/FV_M/scene/2/index.html

2 It seems that school teachers trying to 'eliminate' dialect speech is sadly back in vogue in the UK, under the false pretence that standard English is 'clearer'!

3 Kemp is celebrated in the field of folk song and dance as much as he is pivotal for Shakespearean studies. His ability to hold the stage as a soloist with no need for plot is key here. See Wiles (1987: 24–42).

BIBLIOGRAPHY OF WORKS CITED

Adams, Patch (2007) Private conversation (Dresden, World Parliament of Clowns).

Amsden, Lucy (2015) "The work of a clown is to make the audience burst out laughing": learning clown at École Philippe Gaulier', PhD Thesis (University of Glasgow) http://theses.gla.ac.uk/6372

Bakhtin (1984) *Rabelais and His World* (Indiana: Indiana University Press).

Barker, Clive (1977) *Theatre Games* (London: Methuen).

Belgrad, D. (1998) *The Culture of Spontaneity: Improvisation and the Arts in Postwar America* (Chicago; London: University of Chicago Press).

Benedetti, Jean (1998) *Stanislavski and the Actor* (London: Routledge).

Benedetti, Jean (2008) *Stanislavski: An Introduction* (London: Methuen).

Bogart, Anne and Landau, Tina (2004) *The Viewpoints Book: A Practical Guide to Viewpoints and Composition* (New York: Theatre Communications Group).

Bouissac, Paul (2015) *The Semiotics of Clowns and Clowning – Rituals of Transgression and the Theory of Laughter* (London: Bloomsbury).

Bratton, Jacky and Featherstone, Ann (2006) *The Victorian Clown* (Cambridge: Cambridge University Press).

Brook, Peter (1968) *The Empty Space* (London: McGibbon and Kee).

Carse, James P. (1986) *Finite and Infinite Games* (New York: Random House).

Carson, Christie and Karim-Cooper, Farah (eds) (2008) *Shakespeare's Globe – A Theatrical Experiment* (Cambridge: Cambridge University Press).

Chamberlain, Franc and Yarrow, Ralph (eds) (2002) *Jacques Lecoq and the British Theatre* (Oxford: Routledge).

Coburn, Veronica and Morrison, Sue (2013) *Clown Through Mask* (Chicago: Intellect).

Davis, Andrew (2011) *Baggy Pants Comedy: Burlesque and the Oral Tradition* (Basingstoke: Palgrave Macmillan).

Davison, Jon (2008) 'Draft Notes on Contemporary Clown Research', accessed at: http://jondavison.blogspot.com/2008/01/draft-notes-on-contemporary-clown.html

Davison, Jon (2013) *Clown: Readings in Theatre Practice* (Basingstoke: Palgrave Macmillan).

244 BIBLIOGRAPHY OF WORKS CITED

Davison, Jon (2015) *Clown Training – A Practical Guide* ((Basingstoke: Palgrave Macmillan).

Denis, Dominique (1985) *Le livre du clown* (Strasbourg: Éditions Techniques du Spectacle).

Evans, Mark (2006), *Jacques Copeau* (London: Routledge).

Evans, Mark and Kemp, Rick (eds) (2016) *The Routledge Companion to Jacques Lecoq* (Oxford: Routledge).

Fleming, Cass (2020) 'Playing outside the frame: revealing the hidden contributions of the women in the French tradition of actor training' (*Theatre, Dance and Performance Training*, 11:3, 353–369).

Gaulier, Philippe (2007) *Le gégéneur/The Tormentor* (Paris: Éditions Filmiko).

Grotowski, Jerzy (1969) *Towards a Poor Theatre* (London: Methuen).

Hodge, Alison (2010) *Actor Training* (London: Routledge).

Holdsworth, Nadine (2006) *Joan Littlewood* (London: Routledge)

Holdsworth Nadine (2017) 'Interview', in 'Joan Littlewood Education Pack', accessed at: http://essentialdrama.com/practitioners/joan-littlewood/

Johnstone, Keith (1999, *Improvisation for Storytellers* (London: Faber & Faber).

Kelly, Jon (2015) 'The art of falling over with dignity', in BBC Magazine *Monitor*, 26 February 2015, accessed at: https://www.bbc.co.uk/news/blogs-magazine-monitor-31640227

Kozintsev, Alexander (2010) *The Mirror of Laughter* (New Brunswick: Transaction Publishers).

Krasner, David (2010) 'Strasberg, Adler and Meisner', in Hodge, Alison *Actor Training* (London: Routledge).

Lecoq, Jacques (2000) *The Moving Body: Teaching Creative Theatre* (London: Methuen Drama). (1997) *Le Corps Poétique : un enseignement de la création théâtrale* (Actes Sud); English edition.

Luckett, Sharrell D. and Shaffer, Tia M. (2017) *Black Acting Methods: Critical Approaches* (London: Routledge).

Mamet, David (1998) *True or False: Heresy and Common Sense for the Actor* (London: Faber and Faber).

Meisner, Sanford (1987) *On Acting* (New York: Vintage Books).

Milne, Tom and Goodwin, Clive (1967) 'Working with Joan', in Marowitz, Charles and Trussler, Simon (eds) *Theatre at Work: Playwrights and Productions in Modern British Theatre* (New York: Hill and Wang), pp. 113–22.

Mnouchkine, Ariane and Penchenat Jean-Claude (1971) 'L'aventure du Théâtre du Soleil', in *Preuves*, Paris, 3e trimestre 1971, no. 7.

Murray, Simon (2002) '"Tout Bouge": Jacques Lecoq, Modern Mime and the Zero Body', in Chamberlain, Franc and Yarrow, Ralph (eds) *Jacques Lecoq and the British Theatre* (Oxford: Routledge).

Murray, Simon (2003), *Jacques Lecoq* (London: Routledge).

Ong, Walter (1982) *Orality and Literacy* (London: Routledge).

Opie, Iona and Opie, Peter (1969) *Children's Games in Street and Playground* (Oxford: Oxford University Press).

BIBLIOGRAPHY OF WORKS CITED

Page, Patrick (1997) *150 Comedy Props* (London: Patrick Page).

Preiss, Richard (2014) *Clowning and Authorship in Early Modern Theatre* (Cambridge: Cambridge University Press).

Reddy, Vasudevi (2001) 'Infant clowns: The interpersonal creation of humour in infancy', Enfance, 2001/3 Vol. 53, pp. 247–56.

Rémy, Tristan (1945) *Les Clowns*, (Paris: Grasset).

Rémy, Tristan (1962) *Entrées Clownesques* (Paris: L'Arche).

Rylance, Mark (2008) 'Research, Materials, Craft: Principles of Performance at Shakespeare's Globe', in Carson, Christie and Karim-Cooper, Farah (eds) *Shakespeare's Globe – A Theatrical Experiment* (Cambridge: Cambridge University Press).

Seinfeld, Jerry (1993) 'The Pilot', Part 1, *The Seinfeld Show (Season 4, Episode 23)* (HBO).

Spolin, Viola (1963) *Improvisation for the Theater* (Illinois: North Western University Press).

Tannahill, Jordan (2015) *Theatre of the Unimpressed* (Toronto: Coach House Books).

Towsen, John (1976) *Clowns* (New York: Hawthorne).

Wallis, Mick and Shepherd, Simon (1998) *Studying Plays* (London: Arnold).

Wasson, Sam (2017) *Improv Nation* (New York: Mariner).

Wiles, David (1987) *Shakespeare's Clown* (Cambridge: Cambridge University Press).

Zubok, Vladislav (2011) *Zhivago's Children* (Cambridge, MA: Belknap Press).

INDEX

Adams, Patch 230
AFDA, Johannesburg xiii, 25, 40,
    123, 141
Amsden, Lucy 233
Armin, Robert 210, 224
auguste 22, 197, 198–9, 233, 240

Bakhtin, Mikhail 229
Barker, Clive 235
Benedetti, Jean 227, 228, 235,
    238
Bogart, Anne 228
bouffon 228
Bouissac, Paul 233
Bratton, Jacky 240
Brook, Peter 233

Calgary Clown Festival 107
Carse, James 229
children's games 32, 38, 118, 121,
    200, 241
Circomedia xiv
circus xiv, xv, 2, 4, 22, 55, 90, 100,
    187, 193, 197, 198, 227, 228,
    229, 234, 231, 233–4, 236, 237,
    238, 239
Circus Hub, Nottingham 125
commedia dell'arte 227

dance xiii, 14, 39, 180, 187, 205,
    221–2, 241
Davis, Andrew 239
Denis, Dominique 241

DH Ensemble xiii, 99
drag xiii

Edge Hill University xiv, 177, 239
Estonian Academy of Music and
    Theatre xiv, 209
Evans, Mark 228, 235, 236

Famous Victories of Henry the Fifth,
    The 210–15, 241
Faruq, Jum 97
Featherstone, Ann 240

Gaulier, Philippe 35, 58, 75, 87, 117,
    121, 133, 159, 173, 227, 233,
    240
George Enescu National University
    of Arts, Iaşi xiv
Grotowski, Jerzy 14

improvisation 21, 25, 44–5, 63, 64,
    93, 127, 133, 142, 184, 203, 229

Johnstone, Keith 231

Kemp, Will 210, 216–24
Konijn, Ely 6, 132

Launce 209, 216–24
Lawrence, Thomas (gag book) 240
Lecoq, Jacques xvii, 2, 3, 58, 90–1,
    105, 108, 228, 229, 233, 234,
    237, 238, 239

Littlewood, Joan xvii–xviii
Liverpool John Moores University xiv, 174
London Clown School xiv, 5, 91, 101, 111, 114, 146, 188, 231
London Metropolitan University xii, 5, 111, 114, 154, 171, 238
Luckett, Sharrell D. 10, 229

Mamet, David 6, 232
Marx Brothers 240
Meisner, Sandford 68, 229, 231, 237
Mnouchkine, Ariane 239
Montreal Clown Festival xiii
Monty Python 240
Morecambe and Wise 240
Morrison, Sue 133, 237

New York Clown Theater Festival iv
Ngizwe Youth Theatre xii, 53

Opie, Iona and Peter 241

Page, Patrick 240
Preiss, Richard 100, 235, 237
props 56, 72, 73, 180, 189, 195, 223, 239, 240
puppets xiv, 28–9, 72–3, 97–8, 214

Rastelli 240
Reddy, Vasudevi 231–2, 237
Rémy, Tristan 240
Rose Bruford College xii, xiv, 42, 200, 209, 231

Royal Central School of Speech and Drama xii, 56, 75, 155
Rylance, Mark 100, 234, 235

Seinfeld, Jerry 7–8, 245
Shaffer, Tia M 10, 229
Shakespeare, William xiv, xv, 4, 69, 99, 166, 209, 223, 224, 240, 241
Shakespeare's Globe xiii, 3, 99–100, 234, 235
Shepherd, Simon 240
sketch comedy 133
Spolin, Viola 228
stand-up comedy, 129, 133
Stanislavski, Konstantin xvii, 35, 90, 104, 204, 227, 228, 229, 238
Stellenbosch University xiii, 42
street xv, 100, 187

Tarlton, Richard 210–15, 216, 223, 224, 225, 239, 241
theatre of failure 237
Two Gentlemen of Verona 209

University of the Arts, Cape Town xiii, 169

Victoria & Albert Museum xiii, 56, 169
Vidūṣaka 240

Wallis, Mick 240
whiteface clown 2, 22, 197–9
Wiles, David 241

NOTES **239**

2 Even such conventionalized signals as the raised hand may have no impact, in any case, as I recall one occasion on being part of an audience for a demonstration of a clown workshop: I raised my hand (signal for performers to stop in this case) when they started doing racist clichés, but no-one cared and they carried on – they must have been good clowns, because the teacher was laughing. From this I learned: laughter trumps raised hands.

16 Personal clown skills

1 For example: 'In a state of repose, relaxed, lying on the ground, I ask the students to "wake up for the first time". Once the mask is awake, what can it do? How can it move?' (Lecoq 2000: 40)

2 These were first explored in a research workshop at the clown symposium 'State of Play', held at Edge Hill University in November/December 2018.

3 The original coining of the English word 'clown' combined both the social type (a 'clown' being someone without the urbane knowledge that 'gentlemen' were deemed to possess) and the stage figure (Richard Tarlton being the most well-known of the first English stage clowns from the 1570s onwards). At other points in history, clowns have been closely identified as representations of marginalized 'types', whether by social class or ethnicity, such as the ubiquity of 'ethnic comedy' in the USA in the late nineteenth century (see Andrew Davis 2011: 57–60).

PART THREE 'THAT WAS SUPPOSED TO BE FUNNY'

1 For a wide-ranging and detailed study, see Belgrad 1998.

2 'The reference to circus, which is bound to surface as soon as clowns are mentioned, remains marginal, in my view. As a child, I saw the Fratellini brothers, Grock, the Cairoli trio, Portos and Carletos, all at the Medrano circus in Montmartre, but we were not after this kind of clown at the school. Apart from the comic register, we took no external models, either formal or stylistic, and the students themselves had no knowledge of the clowns I have mentioned. They thus embarked on their research in complete freedom.' (Lecoq 2000: 154)

'Make no mistake; the clowns of Théâtre du Soleil are not real circus clowns. To the latter we have let them keep their gags and their props.' (Mnouchkine and Penchenat 1971: 122)

17 Funny plans

1 See, for example, Thomas Lawrence's gagbook from the 1870s (Bratton and Featherstone 2006).

2 Gaulier writes at length of how clowns are people who think they have great jokes, but which in reality are terrible, and that is the joke: 'You understand? I begin. It's OK. Then, little by little, I flounder. I tie myself in knots. I forget the punch line or say it too soon. The surprise effect is lost. I say I'm sorry I got it wrong. Everyone laughs. Unfortunately they don't laugh at the joke. They laugh at my stupidity.' (2007: 290)

3 The basis for all the gags in Monty Python's sketch, 'History of the Joke', whose humour resides precisely in explaining why and how something is funny.

4 'The "well-made play" is a formula commended by Eugene Scribe to fellow writers and audiences alike in Paris in 1836. Scribe's maxim was that people went to the theatre to be entertained rather than to be improved, and that by picking out elements from past models of dramatic writing – from Ancient Athens through the Renaissance to melodrama – it is possible to arrive at a formula for the delivery for such entertainment: simple action, easily recognizable characters, intrigue and secrets, points of crisis and entanglement, a just conclusion.' (Wallis and Shepherd 1998)

5 The use of rule-based games has become endemic in clown training, especially in the UK. It's worth remembering that clowning is not a sport, but a performance.

6 Such clown props might be either self-built or come from joke shops. See, for example, Patrick Page's *150 Comedy Props* (2007).

18 Intruders

1 The Marx Brothers, Shakespeare, Morecambe and Wise's plays with famous guests, the comic role of Vidūṣaka in the Sanskrit drama, etc.

2 There is a resemblance with the Chair Game with non-obeying clowns, a game I used to introduce the notion of wrongness, as a prelude to devising for performance. (Davison 2015: 100–03)

3 See Tristan Rémy 1945.

4 The long-running act over several generations, of the Rastellis, of which there are numerable iterations on film as here: https://www.youtube.com/watch?v=nZeyr7aKAE8&t=180s

5 See 'The Bottles' as recorded by Rémy, involving three Augustes, a Clown and the ringmaster (1962: 64–71).